# Vegetarian Cooking School Cookbook

**3rd Edition**

by

**Danny and Charise Vierra**

## TEACH Services, Inc.
Brushton, New York

*"Whatever you eat or drink,*
*or whatever you do,*
*do it all for the glory of God."*
**1 Corinthians 10:31**

*Published by*

**TEACH Services, Inc.**
Donivan Road
Route 1 Box 182
Brushton, New York 12916

# VEGETARIAN
## Cooking Schools and Health Lectures

*Learn How to Fight Cancer, Reverse Heart Disease, Lower Cholesterol, Tryglicerides, and Lose Weight, the Healthy and Sensible Way.*

## "NOT A DIET... BUT A LIFESTYLE"

**The four night program includes health lectures on:**
- State of Health in America
- Dangers of Animal Foods
- Benefits of a Vegetarian Diet
- Eight Laws of Health

Cooking Demonstrations, a free cookbook, taste sampling, drawings, and much more!

*Your Hosts:*
*Danny & Charise Vierra owners of Artesian Health Foods II in Tracy, CA and Lodi Health Foods and Back to Eden Vegetarian Cafe in Lodi, CA.*

Danny and Charise are available to conduct their vegetarian cooking school seminars, health lectures, or short talks in your area. For further information on availability, booking a program, or attending a seminar, write or call:
Lodi Health Foods, 521 S. Central Ave., Lodi, CA 95240, (209)368-3168

# ABOUT THE AUTHORS

**D**anny and Charise Vierra are well known throughout the country for their Vegetarian Cooking Schools and Health Lectures. They have conducted their cooking schools before thousands of people over the years, and the demand for their class is increasing. Their nightly lectures include a professional multimedia presentation, video clips, lectures, cooking demonstrations, and taste sampling.

Danny and Charise Vierra

At their cooking schools, Danny energetically presents facts from reliable sources supporting his claims on the state of health in America, the dangers of animal foods and dairy products, the benefits of a vegetarian diet, and the eight laws of health and natural remedies.

Charise, beautiful and charming, cheerfully demonstrates how to prepare vegetarian dishes which are colorful, delicious, and nutritious. The lifestyle they advocate and have lived for ten years is not forced upon anyone, but is offered as a sensible choice to the student with an emphasis on a progressive transition in diet.

The Vierras offer their students what they have discovered to be the best diet for mankind. Says Danny, "The best diet is God's original diet given to Adam and Eve in the Garden of Eden as recorded in the Bible (Genesis 1:29)." It is a vegan diet—a diet free from all animal products. The Creator designed the best possible diet for His creation when he prescribed a diet of fruits, vegetables, grains, nuts, and seeds that contain all the elements necessary for excellent health.

Medical doctors and scientists are just now discovering a wealth of new facts about fruits and vegetables, and their findings are amazing. These foods contain high amounts of antioxidant nutrients and phytochemicals that not only nourish the body and build the immune system, but they prevent cancer, the second leading cause of death in the United States.

Danny and Charise own two health food stores and vegetarian

cafes in California, and Danny is also the director of Modern Manna Ministries, a nonprofit organization that specializes in health and the gospel. Since 1989, Danny has co-hosted a live, call-in radio show called "Healthline" on KCJH Radio (90.1 FM) in Stockton, California. It is one of his eight shows airing throughout the U.S., Asia, Europe, and many other countries. The

> ## "We are medical missionaries, and by God's grace we are sharing His plan with the world!"

Vierras have appeared many times on television, educating thousands of viewers about the health dangers of the standard American diet and the health benefits of God's original diet.

Their greatest testimony is their children, whom Danny refers to as his "Ph.D." in nutrition. Their four children, Giana, Daniel, Lauren, and Mia have never eaten any animal products (other than mother's milk) in their lives. No beef, chicken, fish, cheese, eggs, or cow's milk, and their health is excellent. During their lives only three have had the experience of a single antibiotic, and only one has experienced a doctor visit. Their medical records stand in sharp contrast to that experienced by the average American family with small children. "We have reared our children on God's Plan rather than the 'All-American four basic food groups,' and the rewards are health, energy, and clear minds for each of them," says Charise. "We are medical missionaries, and by God's grace we are sharing His plan with the world," adds Danny.

This unique cookbook contains over 190 of the tastiest vegetarian recipes that the Vierras have found. They would also like to thank their good friend and worker, Rosemarie Nunn, for the wonderful recipes she has donated for this book. The cookbook contains many facts and charts supporting why they choose not to eat animal foods. The main reason, of course, is to maintain optimum health. The book concludes with the eight laws of health which will greatly assist you in the quest for a healthier life. Share this cookbook with your friends. They will find the information and the recipes outstanding.

# CONTENTS

# RECIPES FOR LIVING WELL

# REFERENCES FOR LIVING WELL

# LAWS OF HEALTH

# Guide
# For
# Living Well

## FOOD — MAN'S MEDICINE

*"The doctor of the future will give no medicine, but will interest his patients in the care of the human frame and in the cause of and prevention of disease."*

**Thomas A. Edison**

My personal observation is that what we eat and drink is directly responsible for how we think and feel, and our personal relationship to our Creator. Many times I have talked about the end products of our digestion, and how the metabolism is affected by frequent toxic reactions of food that is poorly digested, perhaps due to overeating, poor combinations and unnatural mixtures of perfectly good food. The symptoms of the diseases that bring on aging and death are only an indication that the systems of our body are not standing up to the abuses of our daily habits. The most irregular and daily habit is that of eating. Thus I would say, look to this avenue for trouble and determine to prevent it.

The all-American diet of hamburgers, hot dogs, potato chips, ice cream and soda pop can hardly be labeled "food," and creates acid residues which are responsible for all kinds of disease.

We should eat to enhance our alkaline reserve, which would include about 50% raw foods—combined simply with other prepared foods that can be easily digested.

Even if not one year was added to our life, the rewards of living, when eating because of health reasons, instead of merely for the gratification of our unnatural appetites, could be enjoyed a hundred fold in physical, mental, and spiritual attainment.

---

*Ten Talents,* Dr. Frank J. Hurd, D.C., and Rosalie Hurd, B.S., pg. 33

## THE STATE OF HEALTH IN AMERICA

- Forty eight million people in the United States suffer from heart disease. This, together with strokes, accounts for nearly half the deaths in this country each year.
- Cancer is the second leading cause of death in the United States.
- Over one million Americans die each year from these two diseases.
- Four out of five persons, age 64 and older, have disabilities or chronic disease.
- In 1945, one out of 15 people died of cancer. In 1971, one in every six deaths was due to cancer. In 1978, after millions of dollars had been spent on conventional methods of therapy, the rate was up to one in every five Americans. Current estimates are that cancer caused one in every four deaths by 1988, and will cause one in every three deaths by 2008.
- American workers lead the world in degenerative diseases.
- In 1987, the U.S. Surgeon General warned that of the 2.1 million Americans who died, nearly 1.5 million were killed by diseases associated with a poor diet.

## DIET FACTS IN THE UNITED STATES

- 62% of Americans are overweight.
- 44 million Americans are considered clinically obese.
- Over half the nation is dieting or has dieted.
- In 1982, 15 billion dollars were spent on weight loss schemes.
- Diets do not work. If they did, why is obesity increasing and new diets constantly being developed?

## CURRENT STATISTICS ON DIET AND DISEASE

- 1961—Journal of American Medical Association reported **a vegetarian diet can prevent 90–97% of heart disease.**
- 1977—In the Senate Report on Nutrition and Human Needs, Dr. Mark Hegsted of the Harvard School of Public Health said, "I wish to stress that there is a great deal of evidence, and it continues to accumulate, which strongly implicates, and in some instances, proves that **the major causes of death and disability in the United States are related to the diet we eat.** I include coronary artery disease which accounts for nearly half of the deaths in the United States, several of the most im-

portant forms of cancer, hypertension, diabetes, and obesity, as well as other chronic diseases."

- 1982—At the National Cancer Institute, doctors said, **"Changing the way we eat could offer some protection against cancer."** NCI has now made diet its number one area of research in cancer prevention.

- 1983—American Cancer Society stated its belief that **"a greater use of fruit and vegetables can significantly reduce a person's risk of developing cancer."**

## ANIMAL DISEASE IS ON THE INCREASE

- Over 100 million chickens die per year of chicken leukemia.[1] About 235 million chickens die each year from all causes — many of which are transmissible to humans.[2]

- Approximately 2½ million beef livers are rejected annually by federal meat inspectors because they have cancer, abscesses or parasitic worms. The rest of the carcass is, however, allowed to be sold for human food.[3]

- Approximately 40 million hogs and piglets die of disease on our farms each year and never (we hope) reach the meat market.[4] About 3¼ million that do reach the slaughter house are rejected in part or total by meat inspectors.[5]

- Over 71 thousand cattle were sold for human food in 1967 after malignant eye tumors were discovered. (Only the eye itself was condemned.)[6]

- Thousands of chickens contaminated or stained with feces are shipped every day instead of being condemned, 81 federal inspectors testified.[7]

- In January 1993, contaminated hamburgers were the cause of the biggest outbreak ever of the deadly bacteria, E. Coli 0157:H7. The outbreak killed four children and hospitalized 500 people.[8]

- In 1993 the USDA temporarily closed 30 beef slaughterhouses after inspections revealed contaminated carcasses at dozens of plants.[9]

- Two cattle diseases, Bovine Immunodeficiency Virus (cow AIDS) and Bovine Leukemia Virus have been discovered in the U.S. BIV and BLV are widespread and suspected of being transmitted to humans through the ingestion pathway.[10]

3

# ANIMAL AGRICULTURE CAUSES ENVIRONMENTAL DAMAGE

- Nearly 40% of the world's grain and nearly 70% of U.S. grain are fed to livestock.

- Almost ½ of the energy used in American agriculture goes into livestock production. It takes the equivalent of 50 gallons of gasoline to produce the red meat and poultry eaten by the typical American each year—and twice that much to process, package, transport, sell, store and cook it.

- Livestock agriculture takes nearly ⅓ of California irrigation water, which amounts to about 190 gallons of water per meat-eating American per day—twice the daily water usage in the average American home.

- Half of the continental United States is used for feedstock, pasture and range. Half of U.S. cropland grows animal feed and hay. This land is eroding quickly. For each pound of red meat, poultry, eggs and milk, farm fields lose five pounds of prime topsoil.

- 270 million acres of public land in the western United States are leased to ranchers for grazing. Already, 10% of this land has been turned into desert by livestock; 70% is severely degraded.

- Livestock produces 158 million tons of waste per year, some of which contaminates underground water tables with nitrates. Animal waste and feed fertilizers account for 40% of the nitrogen and 35% of the phosphorous released into American rivers, lakes and streams.

- Cattle emit ⅓ of a pound of methane for every pound of beef they yield, contributing to the greenhouse effect. This, along with the fuel used in livestock farming, gives every pound of steak the greenhouse warming effect of a 25-mile drive in an American car.[11]

1 *Yearbook of Agriculture*/1956, pp. 466–474

2 *Ibid*, pg. 11

3 *Ibid*, pg. 12

4 *Ibid*, pg. 11

5 *Life and Health*/Oct 1969, pg. 31

6 *Ibid.*/Oct 1969, pg. 31

7 *The Atlanta Constitution*, May 26, 1991.

8 *The Spokesman Review*, January 23, 1993.

9 *The Tallahassee Democrat*, May 28, 1993

10 *Beyond Beef*, Jeremy Rifkin, pg. 143.

11 *Vegetarian Times*/Oct 1991, pg. 68

# Nutritional Guides

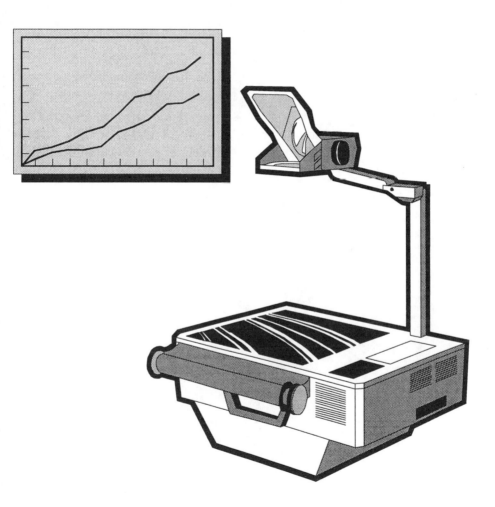

## Facts & Figures

# Notes:

# THE HIGH COST OF
# THE AMERICAN DIET:

- HEART ATTACKS - 125 MILLION
- HIGH BLOOD PRESSURE - 58 MILLION
- OBESITY - 34 MILLION
- OSTEOPOROSIS - 20 MILLION
- DIABETES - 10 MILLION AFFECTED
- DENTAL DISEASES - 95% AFFECTED
- GASTROINTESTINAL DISEASE
- CANCER 900,000 NEW CASES PER YEAR

# FOUR BASIC FOOD GROUPS?
## America's guide to good health

| Sponsored By: | Effects on Children: |
|---|---|
| ■ National Dairy Council | ■ Constipation |
| ■ Kellogg's | ■ Obesity |
| ■ Del Monte | ■ Acne |
| ■ Pillsbury | ■ Rotting Teeth |
| ■ McDonald's | ■ High Blood Pressure |
| ■ Meat Industry | ■ Heart Disease |

Effects are in epidemic proportions!

# CHOLESTEROL:
# ANIMAL VS. VEGETABLE

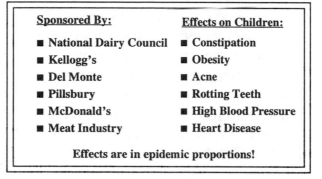

| ANIMAL FOOD: | | PLANT FOOD: | |
|---|---|---|---|
| ■ Egg | 550 | ■ All grains | 0 |
| ■ Kidney , Beef | 375 | ■ All vegetables | 0 |
| ■ Liver, Beef | 300 | ■ All nuts | 0 |
| ■ Butter | 250 | ■ All seeds | 0 |
| ■ Oysters | 200 | ■ All fruits | 0 |
| ■ Cream Cheese | 120 | ■ All legumes | 0 |
| ■ Beefsteak | 70 | ■ All vegetable oils | 0 |
| ■ Lamb | 70 | | |
| ■ Pork | 70 | | |
| ■ Chicken | 60 | | |
| ■ Ice cream | 45 | | |

Cholesterol Content (in Milligrams per 100 Gram Portion)

Pennington, J., Harper and Row, 14th ed., New York 1985

7

# CANCER

## THE STATISTICS:

- SECOND LEADING CAUSE OF DEATH
- 510,000 DEATHS FROM CANCER IN 1990
- 1,400 PEOPLE DIE EVERY DAY
- ONE PERSON DIES EVERY 55 SECONDS
- A NEW CASE EVERY 3O SECONDS
- $20 BILLION SPENT ON RESEARCH
- NO CURE WITH CONVENTIONAL TREATMENTS

## THE RISKS:

- Diet
- Meat & High Fat
- Fried Foods
- Sugar & Junk Foods
- Nitrates & Nitrites
- Aflatoxins
- Drinking Water
- Chemicals & Pesticides
- Food Colorings
- Air Pollution
- Longer Menstruation
- Caffeine
- Alcohol
- Radiation
- Stress
- Cigarettes
- Obesity
- Lack of exercise

## In the prestigious *Advances in Cancer Research*, they conclude:

*"At present, we have overwhelming evidence...(that) none of the risk factors for cancer is...more significant than diet and nutrition."*

## The *Senate Select Committee* wanted an expert opinion on diet and cancer:

*"Nutritional Science is coming of age...No other field of research seems to hold better promise for the prevention and control of cancer and other illnesses, and for securing and maintaining human health...The dietary factors that lead to cancer are principally* <u>meat and fat intake.</u>*"*

Dr. Gio B. Gori  Deputy Dir. of National Cancer Institutes

# THE FATTENING FOODS?
### CALORIE CONCENTRATION (Calories Per Gram)

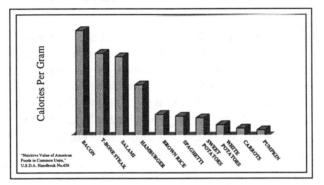

# THE PATTERN IS REMARKABLY PARALLEL

- San Francisco
- England
- Chili
- Brazil
- Mexico
- Guatemala

Journal of the National Cancer Institute, Vol. 51, No. 6, DEC. 1973; and, Foreign Agricultural Circular - Livestock and Meat, U.S.D.A., Washington, D.C., 1976

**BOWEL CANCER DEATHS** (per 100k pop.)

**HEART DISEASE DEATHS** (per 100k pop.)

**PER CAPITA MEAT CONSUMPTION** (kilograms per year.)

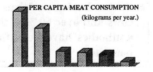

# WHY OUR MEAT SUPPLY IS SO CONTAMINATED:

| HOW THE ANIMALS ARE TREATED: | THE RESULTS OF POOR TREATMENT: |
|---|---|
| ■ Fed contaminated food | ■ No exercise |
| ■ Crowded environments: | ■ Animals die: |
| ◆ Cages | ◆ Stressed animals |
| ◆ Feedlots | ◆ Feces and urine |
| ◆ Trucks | ◆ Develop pneumonia |
| ◆ Holding pens | ◆ Injury - open wounds |
| ■ Hormones | ■ Cancer |
| ■ Antibiotics | ■ Super bugs |

# *60 MINUTES* CONDUCTED A TEST ON SALMONELLOSIS

Over half the birds they purchased from supermarkets were found to be contaminated with salmonellosis. Amazed by the results, they interviewed a number of meat inspectors, who publicly acknowledged on national television the <u>inspection system provides no protection for the consumer.</u>

# BOVINE VIRUSES INFECT HUMAN CELLS

■ Bovine Immunodeficiency Virus - According to the USDA, the cow AIDS virus is widespread among dairy cows and beef cattle, and is suspected of "causing human sera to...become HIV positive." The USDA is continuing its investigations.

■ Bovine Leukemia Virus - Is found in 20% of the cows and over 60% of the herds in the U.S. BLV antibodies have been found in human leukemia patients. Beyond Beef -pg.143, 144

# SUGAR
## Sweet, White and Deadly

- Average American consumes 125 lbs of sugar a year.
- 75% of our sugar intake is hiding where we least expect it: catsup, baby foods, fruit drinks, peanut butter, salad dressings, frozen vegetables, breakfast cereals, mouth wash and toothpaste, to name a few.
- Average American receives approx. 500 nutrition-empty calories a day from sugars.
- It destroys B-vitamins and leaches calcium from the body.
- It affects the nerve and brain functions of the body.

# SUGAR IS ADDICTIVE!

- Causes obesity - which in turn causes hyper-tension, high cholesterol, heart disease and cancer
- Causes one of the most widespread degenerative diseases in America - Tooth decay. 95% of children in this country are affected.
- Contributing factor in diabetes - 1,000 new cases a day
- Causes hypoglycemia (low blood sugar), headache, fatigue, low thyroid, rapid heart rate, depression, poor concentration, lack of HCL.

# AND IF THAT WASN'T ENOUGH:

- Sugar decreases your body's ability to fight infection:

  *Some experts state that there may be as much as a 50% decrease in the ability of certain white blood cells to destroy bacteria after large amounts of sugar have been eaten.*

- Cause of hyperactivity and ADD in children.
- Many of the sugar substitutes are harmful!
- Take this home with you - AVOID REFINED WHITE SUGAR.

11

# COLAS AND SOFT DRINKS

Those who consume colas and soft drinks containing caffeine will subject themselves to the same problems as a coffee drinker.

Soft drinks are especially destructive to children...often causing them to experience irritability, irregular heartbeat, insomnia, hyper-activity, and ADD, just to name a few.

Just drinking one 12oz. can of soda (10-12 tsp. sugar) a day will add 12 pounds of weight to the body a year because of the sugar content.

# SALT

### POSSIBLY THE GREATEST KILLER OF MANKIND!

Salt in the form of sodium chloride is a <u>deadly, poisonous, addicting drug</u> and possibly the greatest killer of mankind!

Most people consume so much salt, that the body can't get all the salt out of the system, so it is carried by the blood and deposited throughout the body in the tissue fluids in an effort to dilute its devastating effects. When a person goes on a fast, he can lose as much as 10 lbs. or more in just a few days from the excessive body fluids retained in an effort to neutralize the salt.

# SALT
## THE SILENT KILLER

- Hardening of the arteries
- Arthritis
- Ulcers
- Distorted Vision
- High Blood Pressure
- Edema
- Cancer
- And other degenerative diseases

# THE DANGERS OF DAIRY
## LEADING CAUSE OF FOOD ALLERGIES:

- **Behavioral**
  - ◆ irritability
  - ◆ restlessness
  - ◆ hyperactivity
  - ◆ headache
  - ◆ fatigue
  - ◆ mental depression
  - ◆ enuresis
  - ◆ muscle pain

- **Skin**
  - ◆ rashes
  - ◆ acne
  - ◆ eczema
  - ◆ seborrhea
  - ◆ hives

- **Blood**
  - ◆ abnormal clotting
  - ◆ iron deficiency anemia

# THE DANGERS OF DAIRY
## LEADING CAUSE OF FOOD ALLERGIES:

- **Gastrointestinal**
  - ◆ canker sores
  - ◆ vomiting
  - ◆ colic
  - ◆ stomach cramps
  - ◆ bloody stools
  - ◆ colitis
  - ◆ malabsorption
  - ◆ diarrhea

- **Respiratory**
  - ◆ nasal stuffiness
  - ◆ runny nose
  - ◆ ear infection
  - ◆ sinusitis
  - ◆ asthma
  - ◆ pulmonary infiltrates
  - ◆ mucus

# "MILK HAS SOMETHING FOR EVERYBODY!"

- Luekemia viruses
- Bovine growth hormone
- Antibiotic residues
- Mad cow disease
- Estrogen
- Xanthine Oxidase
- Protein
- Fat
- Blood & pus
- Cancer
- Increase udder infections
- Resistant bacteria
- Linked to alzheimers
- Breast cancer
- Heart Disease
- Juvenile diabetes
- Adult diabetes
- Yuk!

13

# WHAT ABOUT CALCIUM?

- Most people in the world have diets that contain no dairy products at all.

- Milk is rarely consumed in preindustrial Asian and African societies, yet they have strong bones and teeth and little osteoporosis.

- African Bantu women - a diet free of milk, providing 250-400mg. of calcium from veg. sources, (one half the amount consumed by western women), breast feed 10 babies for 10 months, and osteoporosis is relatively unknown.

# WHAT ABOUT CALCIUM?

- The amount of calcium present in the diet has little effect on the quantity of calcium that is eventually absorbed into the body.

- A high protein diet draws calcium from the bones.

- Unprocessed vegetable foods contain sufficient calcium to meet the needs of adults and growing children.

- Calcium deficiency of a dietary origin is a myth and is virtually unknown in humans.

*TRUE? OR FALSE?*

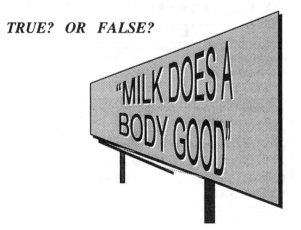

14

# BENEFITS OF
# VEGETARIAN DIETS

- Lower serum cholesterol
- 1/3 risk of developing heart disease
- Less risk of developing cancer
- Less high blood pressure
- Less obesity
- Lower calories
- Higher fiber
- Lower tryglicerides

# ...EVEN MORE BENEFITS

- Fewer bowel problems
- Less expensive
- Better complexion
- More energy
- Less allergies
- Clearer mind and sharper memory
- Less stimulating
- No more bad breath from decaying flesh
- Quick and easy to prepare foods

# THE DIFFERENT TYPES:

<u>STRICT VEGETARIAN OR VEGAN:</u>
*No animal foods of any kind are eaten. All protein is derived entirely from plant sources.*

<u>LACTOVEGETARIAN:</u>
*Animal protein in the form of milk, cheese, and other dairy products is included, but no meat, fish, poultry, or eggs are eaten.*

<u>OVOLACTOVEGETARIAN:</u>
*Animal protein in the form of eggs and dairy products is eaten, but no meat, fish, or poultry.*

15

# PHYTO ISN'T A DOG

> ### phy-to-chem-i-cal
> (fit' o kem'i kəl) n.
>
> Non-nutritive components contained in plant foods, such as fruits, vegetables, grains, and herbs. Thousands of scientific experiments show that phytochemicals exhibit powerful disease prevention capabilities in laboratory animals.

# FRUITS AND VEGETABLES CONTAIN:

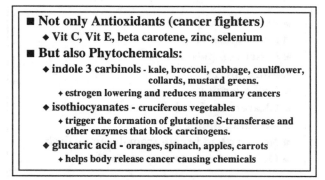

- **Not only Antioxidants (cancer fighters)**
  - Vit C, Vit E, beta carotene, zinc, selenium
- **But also Phytochemicals:**
  - **indole 3 carbinols** - kale, broccoli, cabbage, cauliflower, collards, mustard greens.
    - estrogen lowering and reduces mammary cancers
  - **isothiocyanates** - cruciferous vegetables
    - trigger the formation of glutatione S-transferase and other enzymes that block carcinogens.
  - **glucaric acid** - oranges, spinach, apples, carrots
    - helps body release cancer causing chemicals

# <u>GOOD PHYTO!</u>

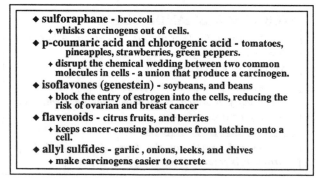

- **sulforaphane** - broccoli
  - whisks carcinogens out of cells.
- **p-coumaric acid and chlorogenic acid** - tomatoes, pineapples, strawberries, green peppers.
  - disrupt the chemical wedding between two common molecules in cells - a union that produce a carcinogen.
- **isoflavones (genestein)** - soybeans, and beans
  - block the entry of estrogen into the cells, reducing the risk of ovarian and breast cancer
- **flavenoids** - citrus fruits, and berries
  - keeps cancer-causing hormones from latching onto a cell.
- **allyl sulfides** - garlic , onions, leeks, and chives
  - make carcinogens easier to excrete

# LETS FACE FACTS:

Everyone knows that we need protein, and that meat, dairy products, and eggs are concentrated protein sources. Few people know that the recommendations to eat these excessive and harmful sources of protein are based on research dealing largely with the nutritional needs of rats. Rats at birth need ten times the amount of protein that a human baby does. The average person living in a modern society consumes enough excess protein every day to produce a mineral imbalance.

# CALORIES FROM PROTEIN

| LEGUMES | |
|---|---|
| Soybean sprouts | 54% |
| Soy flour | 43% |
| Soybeans | 35% |
| Lentils | 29% |
| Split peas | 28% |
| Kidney beans | 26% |
| Navy beans | 26% |
| Lima beans | 26% |

| FRUITS | |
|---|---|
| Lemons | 16% |
| Honeydew melon | 10% |
| Strawberry | 8% |
| Orange | 8% |
| Cherry | 8% |
| Grape | 8% |
| Banana | 5% |
| Apple | 1% |

| VEGETABLES | |
|---|---|
| Spinach | 49% |
| Broccoli | 45% |
| Brussel sprouts | 44% |
| Collards | 43% |
| Cauliflower | 40% |
| Mustard Greens | 39% |
| Mushrooms | 38% |
| Parsley | 34% |
| Lettuce | 34% |
| Green beans | 26% |
| Cabbage | 22% |
| Celery | 21% |
| Eggplant | 21% |
| Tomatoes | 18% |
| Onions | 16% |
| Potatoes | 11% |

| NUTS AND SEEDS | |
|---|---|
| Pumpkin seeds | 21% |
| Peanuts | 18% |
| Sunflower seeds | 17% |
| Almonds | 12% |
| Cashews | 12% |

| GRAINS | |
|---|---|
| Wheat germ | 31% |
| Rye | 20% |
| Wheat, hard rod | 17% |
| Oatmeal | 15% |
| Brown rice | 8% |

*Nutritive Value of American Foods in Common Units U.S.D.A. No. 456*

# AND GOD SAID:

*"Behold, I have given you every herb bearing seed, which is upon the face of all the earth, and every tree yielding seed, to you it shall be for meat."*

*Genesis 1:29*

## COMPARISON OF NUTRIENTS
## IN VEGETARIAN VS ANIMAL FOOD SOURCES

| ITEM | SERVING | PROTEIN | CALCIUM | POTASSIUM | FAT |
|------|---------|---------|---------|-----------|-----|
| Almonds | ¼ cup | 7 grams | 63 mg | 275 mg | 19 grams |
| Beef, Ground | 4 ounces | 18 grams | 10 mg | 258 mg | 15 grams |
| Black Beans, Dry | ½ cup | 22 grams | 135 mg | 1035 mg | .2 gram |
| Blackstrap Molasses | 1 tablespoon | 0 grams | 131 mg | 585 mg | 0 grams |
| Bologna | 4 ounces | 12 grams | 12 mg | 200 mg | 36 grams |
| Chicken Breast | 1 breast | 60 grams | 32 mg | 638 mg | 27 grams |
| Cottage Cheese | 1 cup | 26 grams | 126 mg | 177 mg | 9.45 grams |
| Eggs | 2 whole eggs | 12 grams | 56 mg | 130 mg | 11 grams |
| Figs, Dried | 5 figs | 2.5 grams | 135 mg | 665 mg | 1 gram |
| Kale | ½ cup | 1.1 grams | 45 mg | 150 mg | .2 gram |
| Milk, Lowfat | 1 cup | 16 grams | 297 mg | 377 mg | 4.7 grams |
| Navy Beans, Cooked | ½ cup | 7.5 grams | 45 mg | 385 mg | .1 gram |
| Parsley | ½ cup | 1.1 grams | 61 mg | 218 mg | .2 gram |
| Pineapple Juice | 1 cup | .8 gram | 42 mg | 34 mg | .2 gram |
| Pinto Beans | ½ cup | 23 grams | 129 mg | 935 mg | .1 gram |
| Salmon | 3 ounces | 17 grams | 10 mg | 418 mg | 6 grams |
| Spinach | 1 cup | 2 grams | 51 mg | 259 mg | .2 gram |
| Tofu | 3½ ounces | 8 grams | 100 mg | 0 mg | 4 grams |
| Whole Wheat Bread | 2 slices | 5 grams | 46 mg | 126 mg | 1.4 grams |

NOTE: These statistics are derived from *Nutritional Almanac*, Third Edition, LaVon J. Dunne, pp. 268–304.

Your daily calcium requirements can be met by eating a variety of vegetarian foods. Remember, once you get off the standard high protein American diet, you will absorb more calcium into your system.

# The Vegetarian

## by George E. Vandeman

Fads and bandwagons come and go. A big flash—and then they are gone. Is the present popularity of the vegetarian diet destined to soon fade away like a politician who doesn't quite make it at the ballot box?

Americans, in a growing distrust of the establishment, sent a peanut farmer to the White House. And Washington menus blossomed with peanut dishes—peanut salads, peanut soup, peanut desserts. Peanut butter sandwiches. Even peanut butter milkshakes—which I'm told are delicious.

Then came the jellybean revival. Jellybeans and decorative jellybean containers everywhere.

Now peanuts, in moderation, are good food. But the high sugar content of jellybeans would hardly recommend them for a place in nutrition's hall of fame.

Even so, I would rather trust high-level decisions made over a container of jellybeans than those made in a smoke-filled room. Minds would be a little clearer.

But vegetarianism isn't a fad, and it isn't going to go away. It has survived many a slump and experienced many a revival through the ages.

The earliest record of a vegetarian diet is found in the Bible, in the very first chapter. God said, "I give you every seed-bearing plant on the face of the whole earth and every tree that has fruit with seed in it. They will be yours for food." (Genesis 1:29)

That's interesting. Fruits, grains and nuts. No flesh food. This was the diet chosen by the Creator for the human race.

Let me ask you. If a manufacturer knows best what to put in a car, don't you suppose the Creator knew best what to put into the people He had made?

### LIFESPAN SHORTENED

So there was a time, you see, when everybody on this planet was a vegetarian. And evidently they thrived on it, for those antediluvians had a lifespan of hundreds of years. Adam lived for 930 years, and Methuselah lived 969 years.

It wasn't until after the Flood of Noah's day, when everything had been destroyed and there was literally nothing to eat, that God gave permission for the flesh of animals to be eaten. Even then it was not an unrestricted permission. Only certain animals, which God designated as clean, were to be eaten. And the blood was first to be drained from the carcass.

Did you ever eat a steak without the blood? You'd soon find something else to eat, for it's the blood that gives it the distinctive flavor.

Now the interesting thing is this. Immediately after the Flood, when the human race turned to a diet of flesh food, the lifespan took a nosedive. Is there some connection?

19

## NATION'S DIET PREDICTABLE

"It is interesting," says *Life and Health* magazine, "that the dietary patterns of nations pass through various well-defined stages. When a nation is struggling to grow and its people are poor, the diet is usually frugal, consisting chiefly of plant foods. As prosperity increases, animal foods and wine become more plentiful. Later, self-indulgence and decay set in. Philosophers of every age who observed these trends concluded that they led to the downfall of nations."

## WHAT'S YOUR REACTION?

There's an old story about a science professor in a boy's school. He had an uncanny knowledge of animal life. You could show him the bone of an animal, and he could identify it. Animal life was his world.

One day the boys decided to play a little trick on the professor. They took the skeleton of a bear and stuffed it. Then they sewed over it the skin of a lion. On its head they fastened the horns of a Texas steer, and on its feet they glued the hoofs of a wild buffalo.

They spent a good many nights on the trick, and they did a pretty good job. Then one afternoon when the professor was taking a nap, they tiptoed into his study and set up the monstrosity. And finally, from outside the door, they let out an unearthly growl such as had never been heard before.

Well, the professor woke up, the story says, tumbled off his cot, and stood bolt upright. His reaction was enough to justify all the time they had spent on the trick.

But then, through their peepholes, they saw a surprising thing. The professor rubbed his eyes, looked at the teeth, the horns, and finally at the split hoofs. Then he said, loud enough for the peepholers to hear, "Thank goodness! It's herbivorous, not carnivorous!" And he went back to finish his nap.

How do you react to a person who is a vegetarian? If you're like most people, you probably consider him harmless, even if you do think he is strangely put together—and go back to your nap.

Actress Susan Saint James has an interesting angle. She strongly believes that you can tell a vegetarian by his disposition. She says, "There's a calm that comes over you and a tremendous peace of mind when you're around vegetarians."

## ENDURANCE THE TEST

But you say, "Surely you can't expect a working man to turn out a hard day's work on nothing but bread, bananas and beans."

Well, why not? In the animal kingdom, the real beasts of burden are the ones that eat only plants. The big killer cat is good for short bursts of energy.

It was Teddy Roosevelt who said that if you hitch a lion to a plow, he will fall from exhaustion after one or two times across the field. But the horse can plow all day long!

You see, endurance is the test. And it's carbohydrate, not protein, that gives you staying power. Nutritionists know now that we don't need anywhere near as much protein as was once thought.

Many people have the idea that our bodies are intended for a meat diet, that anything else is somehow strange and unnatural. But nothing could be farther from the truth. The Creator included no flesh food at all in the diet He personally selected and provided for the human race.

## DISEASED MEAT INCREASING

One of the best reasons for being a vegetarian today is the tremendous increase of disease, especially cancer, in animals, in fish and fowl.

And here's something else. Did you ever hear of benzopyrene? In a little over two pounds of charcoal-broiled steak there's as much benzopyrene, a cancer stimulating agent, as in the smoke from six hundred cigarettes.

One more thing. Suppose you have a piece of land. How can you best use it? You can grow food crops for human consumption, or you can grow food for animals and feed the animals to the people. Do you realize that you can feed 14 times as many people with the land if you grow food crops for human consumption?

## VEGETARIANISM NO SACRIFICE

There are, of course, a great many prepared protein foods available today, and many of them are quite ac-ceptable. Our space age technology, especially the spun-fiber technique, has made it possible to approximate both the texture and flavor of meat. These prepared entrees will be a help to you in making a smooth transition to a non-flesh diet.

I think just one meal at our house would convince you that it isn't any sacrifice at all to be a vegetarian. My wife Nellie is a master at preparing light and delicious vegetarian entrees that you would never forget. Put one of them with a baked potato, a green salad, a light dessert, some homemade bread. Well…

I say again it isn't any sacrifice at all to be a vegetarian. It's just another step toward the radiant health you've always wanted—the health God wants you to have.

It's just another step toward an unblemished skin, a new spring in your step, a new light in the eye—toward good blood and untainted breath. It's a step toward untroubled sleep, and a new vigor in the morning.

It's just another step toward an unclouded mind, and clear decision. It's just another step toward being ready for a world where there is no death. No death for anyone. For anything. Ever!

# BIBLICAL LIFE SPANS

**A comparison of the life spans of mankind before the Great Flood when he existed on a VEGETARIAN diet,
with
the life spans after man introduced flesh foods into his diet.**

## BIBLICAL LIFE SPANS

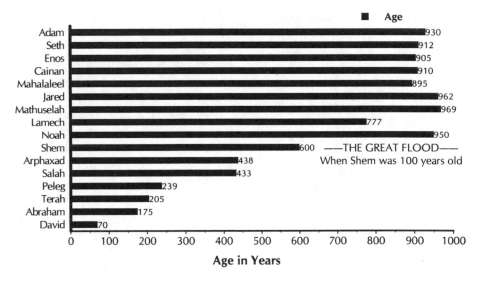

■ Age

| Name | Age |
|------|-----|
| Adam | 930 |
| Seth | 912 |
| Enos | 905 |
| Cainan | 910 |
| Mahalaleel | 895 |
| Jared | 962 |
| Mathuselah | 969 |
| Lamech | 777 |
| Noah | 950 |
| Shem | 600 ——THE GREAT FLOOD—— When Shem was 100 years old |
| Arphaxad | 438 |
| Salah | 433 |
| Peleg | 239 |
| Terah | 205 |
| Abraham | 175 |
| David | 70 |

**Age in Years**

"God said, 'Behold, I have given you every herb bearing seed...and every tree, in the which is the fruit of a tree yielding seed; to you it shall be for meat.'" Genesis 1:29

"The Lord said unto Noah, 'Come thou and all thy house into the ark.... Of every clean beast thou shalt take to thee by sevens...and of beasts that are not clean by two, the male and his female." Genesis 7:1, 2

"And every living substance was destroyed which was upon the ground." Genesis 7:23

# Why were seven needed of each clean animal?

## FOR SACRIFICES

*"Noah built an altar unto the Lord; and took of every clean beast, and of every clean fowl, and offered burnt offerings on the altar."* Genesis 8:20

## FOR FOOD

*"Every moving thing that liveth shall be meat for you; even as the green herb have I given you all things. But flesh with the life thereof, which is the blood thereof, shall ye not eat."* Genesis 9:3, 4

Read Leviticus chapter 11 regarding clean and unclean meats. God prohibited the eating of certain animals because of sanitary reasons—these animals are scavengers.

### HUMANS—HOW ARE WE DESIGNED?

QUESTION: Are we designed to eat flesh meats?
ANSWER: The evidence presented below plainly indicates that we are not.

| CONTRASTING CHARACTERISTICS ||
| HERBIVORE | CARNIVORES |
| --- | --- |
| TEETH—Flat for grinding | TEETH—Designed to tear apart raw meat |
| HANDS—Designed for gathering and picking | CLAWS—Sharp for ripping flesh |
| INTESTINES—24 to 26 feet long: allows time needed for digesting nutrients found in plants | INTESTINES—8 feet long; allows fast digestion of flesh before it putrefies (rots) in the body |
| SALIVA—Contains alpha-amylase: the sole purpose is to digest complex carbohydrates found in plant food | SALIVA—Contains no alpha-amylase |
| HYDROCHLORIC ACID— For digesting protein | HYDROCHLORIC ACID—10 times the amount as Herbivores, needed for meat digestion |

# SHOPPING LIST

**BRAGG'S AMINOS**—Use instead of soy sauce. Bragg's is an unfermented soy product. A good source of amino acids. Can be used in gravies, soups and on vegetables. This is one of our favorites.
*$6.49 / quart*

**ABCO SEASONINGS**—Comes in Chicken, Beef and Vegetable Flavors. Great for soups, stir fry, entrees, etc. Made from natural ingredients.
*$3.25 / pound*

**TEMPEH**—A soybean meatlike product that can be used for sandwiches. Comes in many styles and flavors: barbecue beef, bacon, teriyaki, lemon broil, chili, sloppy joe, and plain. Contains vitamin $B_{12}$.
*$1.79–$2.99*

**TOFU**—High protein soybean curd. Great in place of eggs, cubed in stir fry, or seasoned. Also comes in many varieties.
*$1.25 / pound*

**EDEN SOY, WESTSOY LITE,** or **RICE DREAM**—Excellent milk substitutes. Easy to pour. Use in place of milk in all your recipes, on cereals or just plain. Comes in carob, vanilla or plain.
*$1.49–$2.29 / quart*

**SOYA KAAS CHEESE**—Soy cheese from tofu and soy. Melts, tastes, and looks like real cheese. Use in recipes, sandwiches, etc.
*$5.00 / 12 ounces*

**CAROB**—Chocolate substitute that grows on trees. Great in recipes calling for chocolate powder or chips.
*Approx. $2.00–$3.00 / pound*

**COFFEE SUBSTITUTES**—Roma, Cafix, Sipp, and Cafe du Grain are made from roasted grains, and offer the taste of coffee without the caffeine.

**WHOLE GRAINS**—Barley, corn, millet, rice, rye, triticale, wheat, etc.

**LEGUMES**—Kidney beans, lentils, peas, pinto beans, soybeans, etc.

**FRUIT JUICE SWEETENED**—cereals, cookies, jams / preserves.

**OTHER ITEMS**—Whole wheat flour, whole grain breads, whole grain pastas, nuts, seeds, fruits and vegetables.

\*\*\*\*\*\*\*\*\*\*\*\*\*\*\*\*\*\*\*\*\*\*\*\*\*\*\*\*\*\*\*

**READ LABELS**—Remember to read labels on the foods you buy. We hope that from this class you will realize the "food is food" concept is **out!** Buy foods with the purest ingredients, free from sugars, hydrogenated oils, chemicals and preservatives.

**EAT A VARIETY**—Always eat a variety of foods. Rotate different foods daily. This will assure you all your daily requirements of nutrients. You should not change your diet drastically unless you are willing to follow the principles and guidelines outlined in this class.

24

# Recipes
# for
# Living Well

# Notes:

# Breakfasts

## GRANOLA

12 cups oats
2 cups wheat germ or bran
1 cup cashew pieces
1 cup slivered almonds
1 cup date pieces
1 cup dried pineapple
2 cups whole wheat flour
2 cups shredded coconut
1 cup water
1 cup honey
½ cup oil

Mix all dry ingredients together well. Mix water, honey, and oil in blender. Add to dry ingredients. Mix well. Bake at 250° for 1½ hours in shallow pans, stirring every ½ hour.

## MILLET CEREAL

1 cup millet
4 cups water
½ cup coconut
1 cup apples, chopped
1 cup raisins

Bring water to a boil and add all ingredients except raisins. Cook raisins in ½ cup water for 5 minutes. Pour into millet mixture. Keep on low heat for 45 minutes.

TAPE 1

## DELICIOUS MILLET

1 cup millet
1 cup brown rice
6½ cups water
½ teaspoon sea salt
1 cup crushed pineapple
1 teaspoon vanilla
½ cup coconut
½ cup dates, chopped or pieces
1 cup almonds, chopped

Mix all ingredients in a casserole dish. Cover, and bake for 1–1½ hours at 350°.

## 9 GRAIN CEREAL

2 cups water
1 cup 9 grain cereal
¼ cup dates, chopped or pieces
⅓ cup shredded coconut
¼ cup raisins

Bring water to a boil. Add all ingredients, and stir to combine. Reduce heat and cover. Cook about 7 minutes. Top with slivered almonds and bananas.

## SPECIAL OATMEAL

4¼ cups water
1¾ cups rolled oats
¼ cup wheat germ
8 dates, chopped
½ cup apples, chopped
1 banana

Sprinkle oats in boiling water. Add dates, apples and wheat germ. Cook until done. Slice banana on top.

## APPLE OATS CASSEROLE

2 cups rolled oats
1 cup raisins
1 or more cups unsweetened
    coconut
2 small apples, grated
2 or more cups soy or nut milk
½ cup slivered almonds

*Measurements may vary depending on size of casserole dish.

In an 8 x 8 baking dish, sprinkle ⅓ of the oats on the bottom of dish. Next, layer ½ of the raisins, ½ of the coconut, ⅓ of the oats, and all of the apples. Pour on ½ of the milk. Continue by adding the rest of raisins, oats and coconut. Top with the almonds. Pour on the rest of the milk. Bake at 350° for 30 minutes. Top with Apricot Delicious.

## TAPE 2 APRICOT DELICIOUS

1 16-ounce can apricots or
    peaches
1 16-ounce can unsweetened
    crushed pineapple
2 teaspoons cornstarch

Drain juice from fruit. Mix ¼ cup juice with cornstarch. Add remaining juice and cook until thickened, stirring constantly with whisk. Add fruit and heat. Pour over Apple Oats Casserole before serving.

## APPLE BURRITOS

8 apples, peeled, cored and
    chopped
½ cup softened dates, mashed
    or coarsely blended
½ cup raisins
½ teaspoon maple flavoring
1 teaspoon vanilla

Cook apples in ½ cup water. Add remaining ingredients. Mix well. Roll in whole wheat tortillas and place in baking dish with glaze on top and bottom. (See recipe below). Bake 30–40 minutes at 350°.

## GLAZE

2 cups apple juice concentrate
2 heaping tablespoons
    cornstarch

Cook on high heat until it reaches a glaze consistency, stirring constantly with a whisk.

## MELON MELBA  TAPE 2

1 pkg. frozen raspberries, thawed
1 teaspoon arrow or cornstarch
⅛ teaspoon almond flavoring
3 cups cantaloupe balls or
    chunks
1 tablespoon slivered almonds

The night before, stir cornstarch into berries and cook to thicken slightly. Stir in flavoring. Cover and refrigerate. Prepare melon balls if you have the time, otherwise cut into chunks. Put in serving bowls, cover and refrigerate. When ready to serve, spoon raspberries over melon and top with almonds.

29

## WAFFLES

1 cup millet, whole or flour
1 cup almonds
1 cup cashews
2½ cups "Fearn" Wheat and
    Soya Pancake Mix
3 or 4 cups soy milk (enough
    to make thick batter)

Using a blender, blend 2 cups milk with almonds and cashews. Pour into mixing bowl and add remaining ingredients. Mix and pour onto sprayed hot waffle iron. Makes 16–20 waffles. Top with your favorite syrup, nut butter or fruit topping. Place extra waffles in freezer bags and place in refrigerator. Pop in toaster to reheat.

## CREATIVE WAFFLE
## (Wheat Free)

3 cups milk, soy or rice
⅔ cup cashews
½ cup almonds
⅔ cup dates
½ cup coconut
1 teaspoon vanilla
½ teaspoon salt
1¼ cup Ener G white rice baking
    mix
⅓ cup corn flour
⅓ cup brown rice flour

Blend nuts and dates in milk until they are in small pieces. Pour into a bowl and stir in salt, vanilla, coconut, and flours. Mixture should be fairly thick. Add a touch more milk or flour if needed. Spoon onto a sprayed hot waffle iron. Bake about 8–10 minutes. As batter sits it will absorb moisture and get thicker. Just keep adding a little more milk.

# FRENCH TOAST

1 cup soy or rice milk
1 cup cashews
¾ cup dates
2 tablespoons egg replacer
½ teaspoon sea salt
1 teaspoon vanilla

In a blender combine milk, cashews, and dates. Blend until smooth. While still blending add the rest of the ingredients. Pour into a pie or cake pan. Dip bread on both sides and brown in a lightly oiled skillet. Top with pure maple syrup or your favorite fruit topping. Extra batter may be refrigerated and used later.

# BANANA PECAN CREPES

2 cups water
¾ cup raw cashews
1½ cups rice flour
2 tablespoons honey
¼ teaspoon salt

In a blender, liquefy cashews in 1 cup water. Add rest of ingredients and remaining 1 cup water, and liquefy thoroughly. Let batter stand about 10 minutes. Whiz batter each time you make a crepe. Using a crepe pan or small non-stick skillet, heat on med-high. Spray or brush pan lightly with oil. Coat pan with a thin layer of batter. Cook 2–3 minutes and flip over.

# FILLING

*Can use any fruit you like*

5 - 6 bananas, sliced (or fruit of your choice)
¾ cup pecans, chopped
¼ - ½ cup pure maple syrup

Pour some syrup in pan on medium heat. Add bananas. Cook a few minutes. Add pecans. Fill a crepe, and roll it up. Top with syrup and pecans.

# SCRAMBLED TOFU

1 pound tofu
1 teaspoon onion powder
⅛ teaspoon turmeric
2 tablespoons Bragg's Aminos
1½ teaspoon ABCO Chicken Seasoning

Crumble tofu into frying pan. Stir in seasonings. Cook 5 minutes on medium heat.
Variation: Add chopped bell pepper, onions, or mushrooms

# INDIAN CORN MEAL

1 cup coarse corn meal
4 cups cold water
1 teaspoon salt
2 cups apples, chopped
¼ cup raisins or dates

Stir corn meal into cold water. Cook 15 minutes and add other ingredients. Pour into baking dish and bake at 350° for 45 minutes.

## OLD FASHIONED BREAD PUDDING

6 cups 1-inch bread cubes
½ cup walnuts, coarsely
    chopped
½ cup raisins
1 cup apples, chopped or
    applesauce
4 cups soy or nut milk

Mix ingredients gently in a bowl. Pour into an 8 x 8 lightly oiled baking dish and bake at 350° for 45 minutes.

## FESTIVE FRUIT SALAD

1 whole fresh pineapple,
    chunked or
2 8-ounce cans pineapple
    chunks
4 medium bananas, sliced
3 large oranges, peeled and
    chopped
8 ounces frozen berries (your
    choice)
1 cup unsweetened coconut
2 large kiwi, peeled and sliced
3 apples, peeled, sliced and
    chopped
1 bunch of grapes

Combine and mix gently. Chill.

## BREAKFAST BANANA DELIGHT

½ cup cashews
8 dates, chopped
½ cup water
2 large bananas
1 teaspoon vanilla
½ cup raisins
1½ - 2 cups cooked brown rice,
    millet or oats

Blend first 5 ingredients until smooth. Pour over raisins and grain of your choice, stir to mix. Heat in oven until heated through.

## APPLE BREAKFAST BARS

1½ cups quick rolled oats
¼ cup whole wheat flour
⅔ cups dates, chopped
½ cup walnuts, chopped
½ teaspoon salt
¼ cup orange juice
1½ cups raw apples, shredded

Whiz walnuts with orange juice. Combine all ingredients. Let stand 10 minutes. Press mixture into 8" x 8" baking dish. Bake at 375° until lightly browned, about 25 minutes. Loosen with spatula, and cut into bars while warm. Serve hot for breakfast.

## FRUIT TOPPING

2 cups pineapple juice
8 dates (optional)
3 - 4 tablespoons cornstarch
2 cups unsweetened
    strawberries, peaches or
    other fruit (unsweetened
    frozen fruit is OK)

Blend first 3 ingredients. Boil, and stir constantly. Cool just a little, but before it thickens too much, stir in fruit. This may be refrigerated until the next day. You may also use blueberries with grape juice or apple juice with apples.

## BLUEBERRY TOPPING

2 cups unsweetened pineapple
    juice
3 tablespoons tapioca
2 cups blueberries

Bring pineapple juice and tapioca to a boil. Cook until clear. Stir in blueberries (mashed or left whole), and reheat. Serve over waffles, pancakes, toast.

## GRAPPLE FRUIT SPREAD

1 cup concord grape juice
7 dates
1 cup dried apples
1/4 - 3/4 teaspoon orange and/or
    lemon rind, grated

Soak apples for several hours in grape juice or until soft enough to blend. Blend until smooth.

## BANANA SAUCE

3 ripe bananas
1/2 cup apple juice
1 cup crushed pineapple,
    unsweetened with juice

Combine all ingredients. Whiz until smooth. Delicious over waffles, pancakes, crepes or cereal.

## COCONUT ALMOND MILK

2/3 cup almonds
1/3 cup coconut
1/4 teaspoon salt
1/4 teaspoon vanilla
1 cup water (add to desired
    consistency)

Combine almonds and coconut in dry blender. Whiz until fine. Add salt, vanilla and water. Whiz 1–2 minutes. Strain if desired. Chill.

## SMOOTHIE

1 cup pineapple/coconut juice
1/2 cup apple or orange juice
1 - 2 frozen bananas
1/2 cup frozen strawberries

Pour juices into a blender. Add fruit and blend well.

## NUT MILK

1/2 cup cashews
1/2 cup almonds, blanched
1 quart water
1/4 cup honey
1/2 teaspoon sea salt

Blend all together. Strain if desired. Chill.

## FRUIT MILK

2 cups pineapple or orange
    juice
2 medium bananas

Mix in blender. Serve over cereal in place of milk.

## MULTIVITAMIN-IN-A-CUP SMOOTHIE

Makes 3 servings.

This smoothie will supply most of the vitamins and amino acids you'll need for a day.

    1 cup soymilk
    1 cup fresh orange juice
    1 apple, cored and diced
    3 frozen bananas
    8 frozen peach halves
    1 cup fresh pineapple, diced
    1 mango, peeled and diced (in
        season)
    2 tablespoons wheat germ
    1 tablespoon lecithin granules
    2 tablespoons nutritional yeast

Blend all ingredients together.

## STRAWBERRY / BANANA SHAKE

1½ cups soy or rice milk
¾ cup frozen strawberries
1½ frozen bananas
½ teaspoon vanilla
    maple syrup (to taste)

Whiz all ingredients in a blender. Serve immediately. Shake should be fairly thick.

# Casseroles
# Potpies
# Loaf Entrees

# Notes:

## CASHEW RICE CASSEROLE

1½ cups cashews, ground
1 large onion, chopped and
    steamed
1½ cups bread crumbs
1 cup cooked brown rice
1½ teaspoons garlic powder
½ teaspoon sea salt
3 tablespoons parsley, minced
½ teaspoon sage
¼ teaspoon thyme
1 4-ounce can mushroom pieces
½ cup celery, chopped
1 cup soy or nut milk

Mix all ingredients thoroughly and let stand 10 minutes. Consistency should be fairly thick. You may need to add more liquid or bread crumbs depending upon the texture. Place in a baking dish that has been lightly oiled or sprayed. Bake 40–50 minutes at 350°. Serve with gravy.

TAPE 3 **TOFU CHICKEN**

1 pound firm tofu
¼ - ½ cup brewer's yeast
¼ cup Bragg's Aminos
¼ teaspoon garlic powder
½ teaspoon onion powder

Break tofu in big chunks. If you are making sandwiches cut into strips ¼" thick. Brown in a little olive oil. Remove from pan and place in a bowl. Squirt tofu with Bragg's and sprinkle on rest of the ingredients, stirring to coat tofu evenly. Eat as is with rice and vegetables, make into sandwiches, or fill pita bread. You may eat this warm or cold.

## ZUCCHINI POTATO CASSEROLE

1½ cups bulgur wheat
3 cups water
6 cups zucchini, sliced
3 cups red potatoes, sliced
1 onion, chopped
1 pound firm tofu, crumbled
1½ cups Soya Kaas Cheese,
    shredded
    (Cheddar and Jalapeno)
1 cup tomato paste or Italian
    sauce
2 tablespoons fresh parsley,
    chopped
1 teaspoon basil
1 teaspoon oregano
½ teaspoon thyme
1 teaspoon garlic powder
¼ cup Bragg's Aminos
½ teaspoon salt
    pinch cayenne

Over low heat, cook bulgur wheat in water about 15 minutes. Steam onion and potatoes until almost done. Add zucchini and seasonings. Cook until tender. In a separate bowl, combine bulgur wheat, tomato paste and parsley. Press into the bottom of a casserole dish. Next, combine tofu and ½ of the cheese. Spread on the top of bulgur mixture. When vegetables are done, put them on next. Top with remaining cheese. Bake at 350° for 30 minutes.

## VEGETABLE CASSEROLE

½ pound green beans, fresh
1 medium eggplant, unpeeled,
  cut into 1″ cubes
2 large onions, cut into 1″
  cubes
3 medium carrots, cut into ¾″
  slices on a slant
1 large red or green bell
  pepper,
  seeded and cut into 1″
  squares
2 large stalks celery, cut into
  ½″ slices
2 large potatoes, peeled and
  cut into 1½″ cubes
1 16-ounce can pear-shaped
  tomatoes
¼ cup olive oil or canola oil
½ cup tomato paste
2 teaspoons salt
1½ teaspoons dry basil
¼ teaspoon cayenne pepper
3 small zucchini, cut into ½″
  slices
2 teaspoons honey

Snap ends of beans and cut into 2″ lengths. Combine with eggplant, onions, carrots, celery, bell pepper and potatoes in a large casserole. Chop tomatoes and add to casserole, along with olive oil, tomato paste, salt, basil, cayenne and honey. Stir gently. Cover casserole and bake at 350° for 1½ hours or until vegetables are almost tender, removing lid and basting vegetables with juices about every 30 minutes. Remove casserole from oven and gently mix in zucchini. Return to oven and bake, uncovered, for another 20–30 minutes or until vegetables are tender.

## LAYERED DINNER

6 potatoes, sliced
1 large onion, sliced
2 carrots, sliced
1 green pepper, sliced
1 zucchini, sliced
1 cup corn (frozen or fresh)
1 cup green peas (frozen or
  fresh)

Optional vegetables: mushrooms, broccoli, green beans, etc.

## SAUCE

3 cups tomato sauce
¼ cups Bragg's Aminos
1 teaspoon ground thyme
1 teaspoon basil
2 teaspoons chili powder blend
⅛ teaspoon oregano
⅛ teaspoon sage
2 tablespoons parsley flakes

Layer vegetables in a large casserole dish in order given. Use optional vegetables as desired. Mix ingredients of sauce together. Pour sauce over vegetables. Bake covered at 350° for about 1½ hours.

# PEASANT'S PIE

## TOPPING

4 medium potatoes, cooked
and mashed

Mash potatoes with about ¼ cup
or so soy milk

## SAUCE

2 cups brown gravy or
mushroom gravy or Italian
sauce

## FILLING

1 onion, coarsely chopped
3 carrots, thinly sliced
1 green pepper, diced
½ pound broccoli, cut into
stems and florets
¼ pound green beans, cut into
1-inch pieces
1 bunch spinach, torn into
bite-sized pieces

Steam vegetables (except spinach)
about 15 minutes, until crisp-tender.
Remove from heat. Stir in spinach
and 2 cups gravy. Spoon this filling
into a 9" x 12" baking dish. Spread
mashed potatoes over the top. Sprinkle with a small amount of paprika.
Bake 30 minutes at 350°.

### Helpful Hints

Add ½ pound Brussels sprouts when
they are available. Use favorite vegetables for filling, cut into bite-sized
pieces. Use about 8 cups of chopped
vegetables. If prepared ahead, add
15 minutes to baking time. Use left-
over vegetables, added to others after they have been steamed.

# NOODLE PEAS CASSEROLE

ribbon noodles
cashew milk
ABCO Chicken Seasoning
onion powder
garlic powder
sea salt
peas, uncooked (frozen or
fresh)
mushrooms
cornstarch for thickening

Cook ribbon noodles as directed
on package. Thicken cashew milk.
Season with ABCO Chicken Seasoning, onion powder, a little garlic powder and sea salt. Add peas
and mushrooms. Mix all ingredients well. Bake at 350° until thoroughly heated.

# WALNUT LOAF

2 cups bread crumbs
2 cups cooked brown rice
1 cup walnuts, chopped
1 cup soy milk
½ teaspoon salt
¼ cup Bragg's Aminos
1 onion, finely chopped
1 tablespoon chopped parsley

Mix first 4 ingredients. Add remaining ingredients and mix well.
Put into casserole dish and bake for
1 hour at 350°. Serve with gravy.

## SUNSHINE LOAF

2 cups raw carrots, grated
1½ - 2 cups brown rice, steamed
½ cup peanut butter
1 cup soy or nut milk
½ cup coarse bread crumbs
¼ teaspoon sage
½ teaspoon salt or to taste
1 tablespoon onion powder or
½ cup onions, steamed

Dilute peanut butter with soy or nut milk. Mix nut butter with rice. Add carrots and remaining ingredients, using crumbled bread as necessary to make right consistency. Put into baking dish. Bake 45–55 minutes at 350°. Serve with your favorite gravy.

## VEGETARIAN POT PIE

### DOUGH

2 cups unbleached flour
½ cup whole wheat pastry flour
¼ cup baby oats (coarsely chopped in food processor)
1½ teaspoons sea salt
¾ cup oil
⅔ cup soy milk

Mix all dry ingredients together. In a separate bowl, combine milk and oil, add to dry ingredients. Mix slowly. Dough should be soft and pliable. If it is too dry, add a little more liquid.

### FILLING

2 medium carrots, diced
2 stalks celery, diced
1 large onion, chopped
2 - 3 medium potatoes, diced
½ cup peas
2 tablespoons whole wheat pastry flour
1 cup water
½ teaspoon sea salt
1 tablespoon oil
2 tablespoons baby oats
2 tablespoons ABCO Chicken Seasoning
2 bay leaves

Steam carrot, potato and celery until tender. Add peas and set aside. Sauté onion in oil until soft and transparent. Stir in flour and oats. Add water, seasonings and bay leaves. Heat until mixture has thickened. Stir in vegetables. Remove bay leaves. *(continued)*

Preheat oven to 350°. Roll out the dough to ⅛-inch thick. Cut into desired shapes. Put some filling in the middle and fold in half. Crimp edges. Place on a non-stick cookie sheet. Or if using a pie dish, roll out half the dough and place in bottom of dish. Spoon in filling. Roll out remaining dough and place on top. Crimp edges and make slits on top. Bake for about 45–50 minutes, until the edges are slightly brown.

## CASHEW LENTIL LOAF

1 cup lentils
3 cups water
½ cup onion, chopped
2 cloves garlic, minced
1 tablespoon vegetable oil
⅔ cup carrots, chopped
⅓ cup celery, chopped
2 egg replacers
2 tablespoons whole wheat
    pastry flour
¾ cup raw cashews, chopped
1 teaspoon dried thyme

Cook lentils in water until soft. Cool and set aside. Sauté onion and garlic until onion is translucent. Add carrots and celery. Simmer, covered, 10–15 minutes or until carrots are tender. Allow to cool. Preheat oven to 350°. Mix together lentils, vegetable mixture and remaining ingredients in a large bowl. Spoon into an oiled loaf pan. Bake 45 minutes or until firm. Serve Country Style Gravy over top.

## HARVEST NUT ROAST

2½ cups celery, chopped
3 medium onions, chopped
¾ cup walnuts, chopped
¾ cup pecan or sunflower meal
1½ teaspoons salt
2 - 2½ cups soy milk
1¼ teaspoon sweet basil leaves
½ teaspoon sage
3 cups bread crumbs

Steam celery and onions. Combine remaining ingredients, folding in bread crumbs last. Place in loaf pan sprayed with non-stick spray, and bake for 1¼ hours at 350°. Loaf may have to be covered with foil near the end of baking if top begins to get too brown. Tastes good served with Country Style Gravy.

## POLENTA

3 cups water
1½ teaspoon sea salt
1 small potato, diced small
1 cup polenta flour
1 cup cold water

Bring to a boil in large sauce pan first 3 ingredients. Gradually stir in a mixture of 1 cup cold water, 1 cup polenta. Continue boiling on medium heat stirring constantly until mixture thickens. Lower heat, cover, cook slowly for 10 minutes or more until done. Stir a few times while cooking the last 10 minutes. Good plain or with your favorite sauce and vegetables on top or broiled the next day.

## STUFFED GRAPE LEAVES

¼ cup olive oil
¼ cup pine nuts
2 large onions, chopped
½ parsley, chopped
2 cups cooked rice
2 tablespoons water
4 teaspoons dill weed
½ teaspoon salt
⅛ teaspoon cayenne pepper
1 tablespoon fresh lemon juice
40 small grape leaves or 1 jar

Heat oil in a wide frying pan over medium heat. Add nuts and cook, stirring until golden. Remove nuts and set aside. Add onions and cook, stirring frequently, until golden brown. Add parsley and cook for 2 minutes. Remove pan from heat and stir in rice, dill, salt, cayenne and lemon juice. Stir gently to blend. Drain grape leaves and rinse with cold water. Drain again. Spread leaves, veined side up, on a flat surface. Cut off stems. Place 1 tablespoon of filling near stem end, fold sides in and roll up. Arrange filled leaves, seam side down, in a single layer, in a baking pan. Sprinkle with water and bake covered at 350° for 25 minutes.

## CABBAGE ROLLS

1 medium onion, finely
    chopped
1 clove garlic, minced
1 tablespoon oil
1 medium carrot, diced
1 large stalk celery, diced
12 - 14 cabbage leaves
½ teaspoon ground coriander
    seed
¼ cup water
3 cups cooked rice
2 tablespoons Bragg's Aminos
¼ cup filberts or almonds,
    toasted and chopped
1 cup soy jack cheese,
    shredded (optional)
⅓ cup soy parmesan cheese
    (optional)
1 pound fresh mushrooms,
    sliced (optional)

Sauté onion and garlic in oil for 2–3 minutes. (Optional: add shredded soy jack cheese, and soy parmesan cheese. You can also add 1 pound fresh sliced mushrooms. Sauté them with onion and garlic). Add carrot, celery and coriander. Sauté briefly, then add water. Bring to a boil and cover. Cook over low heat for 3 minutes, then stir in rice, Bragg's and nuts. Wash cabbage leaves carefully, and steam in a large pot for no more than 3 minutes. Cut out the inflexible central stem from each leaf. *(continued)*

Preheat oven to 350°, place ⅓ cup of filling on each leaf. Roll the leaf around it lengthwise into a fat little pocket, tucking in the sides as you roll. Place the rolls in a baking dish, pour marinara sauce over, and bake covered for 30 minutes. Uncover and continue baking for another 10–15 minutes.

## TOFU TURKEY ROAST

5 lbs. firm tofu, crumbled fine
5 tablespoons veg. chicken
    flavor seasoning.
3 tablespoons brewer's yeast
½ cup Bragg's Aminos
2 teaspoons sage
12 - 16 cups stuffing (about 2
    packages)

Mix all ingredients together except stuffing. Line an 11¾" colander with cheese cloth. Transfer tofu into colander. Press tofu evenly around all sides and bottom. Fold edges of cheese cloth over it. Place a bowl over the surface of the tofu and weigh it down with a heavy object to press the liquid from the tofu—about one hour. Prepare your favorite stuffing recipe and set aside. After tofu has set 1 hour, hollow out tofu turkey within one inch thickness. Pack in stuffing and cover with remaining tofu. Pat down so that surfaces are firm and flat.

Place an oiled baking sheet on top of colander then flip turkey over. Remove cheese cloth. Bast with

toasted sesame oil and Bragg's Aminos. Cover with foil and bake at 400° for 1 hour. Remove foil, baste again and return to oven to bake for approximately 1 more hour or until golden brown. Serve with your favorite gravy.

## ✳ ENCHILADA CASSEROLE

2 cans (16oz.) kidney beans,
    undrained
½ cup chopped red onion or
    scallion
1 tablespoon chili powder
1 teaspoon garlic, minced
1 teaspoon cumin
1 dozen corn tortillas
1 can (11oz.) whole kernel
    corn, undrained
1 can (4 oz.) chopped green
    chilies
2 tablespoons chopped cilantro
1 can (14½ oz.) chopped
    Mexican stewed tomatoes,
    undrained
1 recipe Cashew Pimento
    Cheese (pg. 84)

In a bowl mash, kidney beans, onions, garlic, and seasonings. In a casserole dish, layer 4 corn tortillas, ½ of the beans, ⅓ of the cheese, 4 more tortillas, remaining beans, all tomatoes, remaining cheese. Cover with foil and bake at 350° for 35–40 minutes. Serve with soy Sour Cream, chopped green onions, or chives and sliced olives.

# Notes:

# Pastas & Pizza

# PIZZA

## SAUCE

2 cups tomato sauce
1½ cups tomato paste
1 teaspoon onion powder
½ teaspoon basil
½ teaspoon oregano
½ teaspoon garlic powder

Combine all ingredients in a saucepan and simmer over low heat about 15 minutes to blend flavors.

## HELPFUL HINTS

Use as a pizza sauce, as a sandwich spread, or as a catsup substitute. Will keep in refrigerate for several weeks.

### CRUST (by hand)

1½ teaspoons active dry yeast
1½ cups hot water
2 tablespoons honey
3¾ cups whole wheat flour
    (may use ½ unbleached
    flour)
1 teaspoon sea salt
2 tablespoons olive oil

Mix the yeast and honey in the hot water (110°). Let stand 10 minutes. Stir in salt, oil and flour, 1 cup at a time. Mix well. Knead dough in bowl about 50 times. Let rise 1 hour. Roll out onto pizza pan. Poke holes in crust to let air escape, and prebake 10 minutes at 400°. Top with sauce, soy cheese and vegetables. Bake 25–30 minutes at 350°

### CRUST (by Bosch)

5 - 7 cups unbleached white
    flour
5 - 7 cups whole wheat flour
7 cups hot water
⅔ cup oil
¼ cup honey
2 tablespoons yeast
2 tablespoons sea salt

In a blender, combine 1 cup hot water, honey and yeast. Let stand 10–15 minutes. Pour into Bosch bowl. Add salt and oil. Mix on speed #1 for a second. Add 5 cups hot water and about 4 cups flour. Turn machine on. Add remaining flour, 1 cup at a time. Continue mixing until dough pulls away from the sides. This should take about 5 minutes. Keep mixing for 10 minutes. If you are making bread, form into loaves, set it in pans, let it sit about 15 minutes, until it starts rising. Then put it into preheated 350° oven. Bake 45–55 minutes. For pizza, roll out onto pizza pan. Poke holes with fork. Prebake 10 minutes at 400°. Top with sauce, soy cheese and vegetables. Bake 25–30 minutes at 350°.

## MACARONI WITH CASHEW PIMIENTO CHEESE

2 cups macaroni noodles
(whole wheat, sesame or
any other)
2 cups water
1 cup cashews, rinsed
2 tablespoons lemon juice
1 teaspoon onion powder
½ teaspoon garlic powder
1 4-ounce jar pimientos
1 teaspoon salt
1½ cups bread crumbs, soft

### MACARONI

Bring 2 quarts of water to boil with 1 teaspoon salt. Add 2 cups macaroni. Boil until tender.

### SAUCE

Blend until smooth **1 cup** water and the remaining ingredients (except bread crumbs). Now add remaining 1 cup water.

Place drained and rinsed macaroni in flat casserole dish. Pour sauce over macaroni. Cover and bake 30 minutes at 350°. Uncover and top with soft bread crumbs or cubes. Bake for another 15 minutes. Serves 6–8.

## VEGETABLE LASAGNA

1 onion, chopped
1 bell pepper, chopped
2 zucchini, quartered and
sliced
1 pound firm tofu
2½ cups mozzarella soy cheese
9 lasagna noodles, cooked
4 cups (approx) Italian sauce
(pg. 49)
1 teaspoon garlic powder
2 tablespoons honey

Sauté onion and bell pepper until almost done. Add zucchini. Cook until all vegetables are done. In another pan, crumble tofu and sauté in a little olive oil. Sprinkle with garlic powder and honey. In casserole dish, spread some sauce on bottom, then layer noodles, crumbled tofu, vegetables, cheese, and more sauce. Repeat procedure ending with noodles, sauce, and top with cheese. You will have two layers of tofu and vegetables. Bake for 35 minutes at 350°.

*Another way to do the filling is to mix the sautéed vegetables, browned tofu, and cheese all together in a bowl. As cheese melts due to the hot vegetables and tofu, mixture will get creamy, like ricotta cheese.

## "CHICKEN" CACCIATORE

1 8-ounce package Heartline
    Chicken Fillet
1 large onion, chopped
1 bell pepper, chopped
2 cloves garlic, minced
1 15-ounce can tomato sauce
1 teaspoon sea salt
¼ teaspoon thyme
1 teaspoon oregano leaves
⅛ teaspoon cayenne
    olive oil

Add 1 cup of water to each cup of Heartline (enough water to completely cover). Boil Heartline for 10 minutes or more to desired texture. In a frying pan, sauté bell pepper and onion in olive oil. Add Heartline Chicken, tomato sauce and seasonings. Simmer about 10–20 minutes. Serve over brown rice.

TAPE
3

## FETTUCCINE ALFREDO

3 cups water
½ cup cashews, blanched
5- 4 tablespoons soy parmesan
    cheese
¾ ½ teaspoon sea salt
3- 2 tablespoons flour or cornstarch
½ teaspoon garlic powder
1 onion, minced
4 cloves garlic, minced

Blend ½ cup water with cashews until smooth. Add the remaining water and ingredients, except onion and garlic. Saute' onion and garlic until soft. Then add to cream sauce and heat until thickened stirring with a whisk.

Steam until crisp tender:

broccoli
cauliflower
red bell pepper
carrots
zucchini

Cook 1 pound package of fettuccine or a pasta of your choice. Put veggies over pasta, then pour on cream sauce.

## TOFU LASAGNA

1 pound firm tofu
1 package Soya Kaas
    Mozzarella Cheese
3 tablespoons Soyco Parmesan
    Cheese
3 tablespoons dried parsley
1 teaspoon garlic powder
    Italian sauce
    lasagna noodles

Crumble tofu and add 1 cup shredded cheese, plus all the rest of the ingredients, including about 1½ cups of sauce. Pour some sauce in a casserole dish, then a layer of noodles and a layer of tofu mixture. Sprinkle on some cheese. Continue the procedure ending with cheese. Bake at 350° for 30 minutes.

## MANICOTTI

1 box manicotti noodles
1 pound firm tofu
1 package of Soya Kaas
    Mozzarella Cheese
3 - 4 cups spaghetti sauce
1 tablespoon dried parsley
1 teaspoon garlic powder
½ teaspoon sea salt

Cook manicotti noodles according to directions on box. Mix tofu with dried parsley, garlic powder, ½ cup spaghetti sauce, and 1 cup of mozzarella cheese. Stuff noodles with tofu mixture. Spread some spaghetti sauce on bottom of casserole dish. Layer stuffed manicotti noodles in dish. Pour spaghetti sauce over top of noodles, then cover with rest of grated cheese. Bake for 20 minutes at 350°.

## ITALIAN SAUCE

1 onion, chopped
3 cloves garlic, minced
3 tablespoons fresh parsley,
    chopped
6 cups crushed tomatoes in
    puree
1½ cups tomato paste
1½ teaspoons sea salt
1 tablespoon basil
½ tablespoon oregano
4 tablespoons honey

Sauté onion, garlic and parsley until limp. Add all remaining ingredients and simmer for ½ hour, stirring frequently.

## TEMPEH CACCIATORE

1 medium onion, slivered
½ cup green bell pepper,
    chopped
2 tablespoons olive oil
1 clove garlic, minced
1 cup fresh mushrooms, sliced
2½ cups tomatoes, peeled and
    chopped or
1 15-ounce can whole
    tomatoes, chopped
1 bay leaf
½ teaspoon oregano
1 teaspoon basil
8 ounces tempeh, cubed
2 tablespoons Bragg's Aminos
½ cup tomato juice
4 cups brown rice, cooked

Sauté onion and bell pepper in 1 tablespoon olive oil over low heat until onion is translucent. Then stir in garlic and mushrooms, and cook another 5 minutes or so. Add tomatoes, juice, bay leaf, oregano and basil. Bring to a boil. Reduce heat and simmer for 10 minutes.

In another small skillet or wok, sauté tempeh in remaining tablespoon of oil, stirring frequently, until it browns slightly. Transfer tempeh to sauce, add Bragg's, and simmer over low heat for at least half an hour. Remove and discard bay leaf. Serve tempeh mixture over rice or spaghetti. Serves 4.

## CANNELLONI

2 bunches fresh spinach
1 large onion, chopped
2 zucchini, quartered
1 pound firm tofu
1½ cups Soya Kaas Mozzarella
    Cheese (reserve ½ cup for
    topping)
3 tablespoons fresh parsley
2 cloves garlic, minced
4 tablespoons bread crumbs
4 tablespoons soy parmesan
    cheese
1 teaspoon basil
1 teaspoon oregano
1 cup mushrooms
3 - 4 cups Italian sauce (pg. 49)
1 box cannelloni or manicotti
    noodles

Clean and steam spinach. Sauté onion, zucchini, garlic and parsley. In a bowl, crumble tofu very fine. Add vegetables and all other ingredients except sauce. Mix well. Stuff cooked noodles with mixture. Pour Italian sauce on the bottom of casserole dish. Place cannelloni in dish and cover with more sauce. Top with mozzarella cheese, mushrooms and parmesan cheese. Bake at 350° for 30 minutes. After baking is done, sprinkle with fresh chopped parsley.

## EGGPLANT PARMESAN

1 eggplant or large zucchini
    (3–4″ dia.)
1 cup Soya Kaas Mozzarella
    cheese
2 tablespoons soy parmesan
    cheese
3 cups Italian sauce (p. 49)

Mix together in a shallow container:
1½ cups bread crumbs
½ cup whole wheat pastry flour
1 teaspoon onion powder
½ teaspoon garlic powder
½ teaspoon sea salt

In a separate shallow container, mix:
½ cup egg replacer
¾ cup water

Peel and slice eggplant in ½″ slices. If doing zucchini, do not peel. Steam until crisp tender. Do not overcook. Dip slices first in egg replacer mixture (both sides), then in bread crumb mixture. Brown on both sides in skillet. Pour some Italian sauce in bottom of casserole dish. Place browned slices in dish overlapping, if necessary. Spoon on more sauce, sprinkle with mozzarella cheese and parmesan cheese. Put in oven for about 10 minutes or until cheese melts. If using zucchini, I usually use the ones from our garden that have gotten rather large. Using smaller ones is more time consuming.

# Chinese Dishes

# Notes:

## CASHEW CHOW MEIN

1 onion, chopped
3 stalks celery, chopped
2 cups mushrooms, fresh or
　canned
1 cup firm tofu, cubed
3 cups cooked whole grain flat
　noodles (Udon noodles
　work well)
1 cup cashews, rinsed and
　roasted
2 tablespoons onion powder
2 cups mushroom soup (recipe
　below)
2 teaspoons salt

Sauté onion, celery and mushrooms in 3 tablespoons oil and 3 tablespoons water. Add tofu. Add remaining ingredients and pour into casserole dish. Bake at 350° for 25 minutes.

## QUICK MUSHROOM SOUP

½ cup canned mushrooms
2 tablespoons unbleached
　white or
　whole wheat pastry flour
1½ teaspoons ABCO Chicken
　Seasoning
½ cup water
1½ cups soy milk
1 teaspoon dry parsley flakes
½ teaspoon salt

Blend briefly until mushrooms are cut in pieces, not smooth. Pour into saucepan and cook over low heat until thickened. Stir constantly.

## EGG ROLLS

1 onion, chopped
2 cloves garlic, minced
2 cups bean sprouts
2 cups shredded cabbage
1 cup carrot, grated
1 sweet potato, grated
2 - 3 teaspoons Bragg's Aminos
12 - 15 corn tortillas

Sauté onion and garlic until limp. Add the rest of the ingredients and cook until tender. Do not overcook. Fill soft and warm tortillas with mixture. Place seam side down in baking dish. Put in 350° oven to warm. Sweet and Sour Sauce may be used on top.

## STIR FRY VEGGIES

1 red onion, sliced into half
　rings
3 zucchini, sliced
1 bell pepper, chopped
3 carrots, sliced
2 tablespoons olive oil
　(optional)
2½ teaspoons garlic powder
3 tablespoons ABCO Chicken
　Seasoning
¼ cup Bragg's Aminos
　Other vegetables of your
　choice

Sauté onion and carrots 2–3 minutes in oil or water in fry pan or wok. Add remaining vegetables. Stir around and add seasonings. Cook until tender.

# TOFU AND VEGETABLES WITH SWEET AND SOUR SAUCE

## SAUCE

1 cup tomato sauce
1 cup unsweetened pineapple juice
¼ cup honey
½ teaspoon salt
1 teaspoon Bragg's Aminos
3 tablespoons lemon juice
¼ cup crushed pineapple
1½ tablespoons cornstarch

Combine all ingredients except cornstarch, and bring to a boil. Mix cornstarch with a little water and add to mixture. Heat until thickened, stirring constantly with a whisk.

## VEGETABLES

3 stalks celery, sliced
3 carrots, sliced
1 onion, chopped
1 bell pepper, chopped
2 zucchini, sliced
1 can water chestnuts
1 can bamboo shoots
2 tablespoons Bragg's Aminos
½ teaspoon garlic powder

Sauté celery, onion, carrot and bell pepper in small amount of water. Add zucchini, water chestnuts and bamboo shoots. Sauté with Bragg's Aminos and garlic powder until vegetables are done.

## TOFU

1 pound firm tofu
1 tablespoon olive oil
2 tablespoons Bragg's Aminos
1 teaspoon garlic powder
1 tablespoon honey

Cut tofu into cubes and brown in a non-stick pan with a tablespoon or so of olive oil. Add Bragg's Aminos, garlic powder, and honey. Cook until edges are slightly browned. Add tofu to vegetables. Spoon over brown rice. Top with sauce.

# Mexican Entrees

# Notes:

## ENCHILADAS

1 pkg. whole wheat or corn
   tortillas
2 cups brown rice, cooked
6 cups pinto beans, cooked
   and mashed
1 cup olives
2 cups Soya Kaas Cheese
1½ cups salsa
1 teaspoon garlic powder
2 teaspoons onion powder
2 teaspoons sea salt
2 teaspoons cumin
1 tablespoon Grandma's Chili
   seasoning
   Enchilada Sauce (see below)

Mix all ingredients (to taste). Fill tortillas. Pour some enchilada sauce on bottom of casserole dish. Lay filled tortillas seam side down. Top with sauce and cheese. Bake until hot (20–30 minutes) at 350°.

## ENCHILADA SAUCE

2 cups crushed tomatoes in
   puree or
2 cups tomato sauce
2 cups water
¼ cup flour or
2 tablespoons cornstarch
2 tablespoons chicken seasoning
2 teaspoons chili powder
1 teaspoon garlic powder
1 teaspoon onion powder
½ teaspoon cumin

Blend all ingredients (except tomatoes) in a blender. Pour blended mix into a saucepan, and add to-matoes. Heat until thickened, stirring constantly with a whisk.

## VEGETABLE ENCHILADAS

1 onion, chopped
1 bell pepper, chopped
2 zucchini, quartered and sliced
2 cups eggplant, peeled and
   diced
4 tablespoons fresh cilantro,
   chopped (reserve 2
   tablespoons for top)
½ teaspoon sea salt
1 teaspoon garlic powder
1 teaspoon cumin
1 teaspoon Grandma's Chili
   Seasoning
2 - 3 cups salsa or enchilada
   sauce
   fresh corn tortillas
   Soya Kaas Cheese (optional)

Sauté onion, bell pepper and egg-plant until almost done. Add zucchini and seasonings. Cook until tender. Pour some salsa on the bottom of a casserole dish. Fill tortillas with vegetables, and roll them up. Place seam side down. Cover with salsa and sprinkle with soy cheese if desired. Bake 20–30 minutes at 350°, then top with cilantro.

## TOFU-SPINACH ENCHILADAS

1 onion, chopped
2 cloves garlic, minced
½ - 1 cup mushrooms, sliced
2 bunches fresh spinach, chopped or
1 package frozen spinach, thawed and drained
½ teaspoon salt
½ teaspoon garlic powder
1 pound firm tofu
  enchilada sauce (see recipe, pg. 57)
  Cashew Pimiento Cheese (pg. 84) or Soya Kaas Cheese

Sauté garlic cloves and onions until onions are transparent. Add mushrooms, tofu and seasonings. Cook 1 minute, then remove from heat. Stir in spinach. Fill each tortilla with 3 tablespoons vegetable filling. Roll and put into baking pan. Cover with enchilada sauce, then top with cashew pimiento cheese spread. Bake at 350° until aroma is irresistible, 20–30 minutes.

## GREEN ENCHILADAS

1 tablespoon oil
2 large onions, chopped
¼ teaspoon salt
12 corn tortillas
3 cups soy cheese, shredded
1 cup soy sour cream (homemade or store bought) (recipe, pg. 86)
1 package cream of mushroom soup
1 10-ounce package frozen chopped spinach, thawed
2 green onions (including tops) sliced
1 4-ounce can diced green chili peppers

Heat the oil (or use water) in a wide frying pan over medium heat. Add onions and cook until soft (about 5 minutes). Stir in salt, then set pan aside. Across the middle of each tortilla, sprinkle 2 tablespoons cooked onion and shredded cheese. Roll to enclose. Place tortillas, seam side down, in a greased, shallow 9 x 13 inch baking pan.

### SAUCE
Squeeze spinach to remove excess moisture. In a blender or food processor, puree spinach, green onions, chili peppers, soup and sour cream until smooth. Pour mixture over tortillas. Sprinkle remaining cheese over all. Bake uncovered at 350° for 30 minutes, or until hot and bubbly.

## TAMALE PIE

½ package soft tofu
4 green onions
1 can corn, undrained
1 can green beans, drained
1 can stewed tomatoes
1 cup fine corn meal
1 can sliced olives
2 tablespoons lemon juice
1 tablespoon chili powder
1 tablespoon honey
½ teaspoon cumin
½ teaspoon garlic powder

Sauté green onions. Blend tofu, lemon juice and honey in a blender. Mix all ingredients in a bowl. Pour into a casserole dish. Sprinkle Soy Kaas Cheese on top. Bake 35 minutes at 350°. Serves 5–6.

## TACOS

Cedar Lake Sloppy Joe Mix
Grandma's Chili Seasoning
onion powder
garlic powder
Soya Kaas Cheese
lettuce
onion
avocado, sliced
salsa
taco shells

Heat sloppy joe mix. Add chili seasoning, onion powder and garlic powder to taste, then spoon into taco shells. Add cheese, onion, lettuce, avocado and salsa.

## BLACK BEAN CHILI BURRITOS

2 cups dry black beans
1 large onion, chopped
1 large bell pepper, chopped
3 cloves garlic, minced
⅓ cup cilantro, chopped
1 teaspoon chili powder
2 teaspoons cumin
2 15-ounce cans Mexican
   stewed tomatoes or 3½
   cups fresh tomatoes
1 tablespoon honey
1 teaspoon sea salt
   Soya Kaas Cheese
   Tempeh, cubed (optional)
   cooked rice
   olives
   tortillas

Soak beans overnight. The next morning change water and cook beans with sea salt until tender, about 2 hours. Drain water from beans. Sauté onion and bell pepper, honey and seasonings. Add tomatoes and cilantro. Mash down tomatoes. Add beans and mash down. (Potato masher works well). Fill tortillas with chili, Soya Kaas Cheese, tempeh, and rice. Eat as is, or top with salsa, shredded lettuce, soy sour cream, guacamole, soy cheese, and olives. Also tastes great as a dip with tortilla chips, or in taco salad.

## GARDEN TACOS

2 cups cooked brown rice
1 cup cooked lentils
1 onion, chopped
1 bell pepper, chopped
1 cup celery, chopped
2 cups zucchini, quartered and
    sliced
1 15-ounce can Mexican
    stewed tomatoes
3 cloves garlic, minced
2 teaspoons chili seasoning

Sauté all vegetables and garlic until tender. Add rice, lentils and seasonings. Simmer until flavors are absorbed. Fill corn tortillas with mixture and add your favorite toppings: lettuce, salsa, avocado, onion, etc.

## MEXICAN TOFU CASSEROLE

1 onion
2 pounds firm tofu
1½ tablespoons ABCO Chicken
    Seasoning
2 teaspoons cumin
1 teaspoon turmeric
½ can Ortega chilies
1 3.8-ounce can sliced
    black olives
1 28-ounce can tomato sauce
    Corn tortilla chips
    Soya Kaas Cheese, shredded

Sauté onion in small amount of olive oil. Crumble in tofu. Add seasonings and blend well. Add olives and chilies. Pour a portion of tomato sauce into glass casserole dish. Crumble chips on next. Layer ¼ of tofu mixture on next. Pour more sauce, chips and tofu. Continue layering. Top with shredded soy cheese. Bake 35 minutes at 350°.

## PAELLA
## WITH SAFFRON RICE

1 onion, chopped or sliced
1 red bell pepper, sliced
1 green bell pepper, sliced
4 stalks celery, sliced
  pinch sea salt
1 can Mexican stewed tomatoes
½ teaspoon chili powder
1 pound Lemon Broil Tempeh, cubed
½ cup arame seaweed (optional)

Sauté onion, bell peppers, celery and salt. When vegetables are just about done, add stewed tomatoes and chili powder. Bake Tempeh until brown. Add to vegetable mixture. Add seaweed. Cook 5–10 minutes more. Serve over rice.

### RICE

2 cups water
1 cup brown basmati rice
½ teaspoon turmeric
½ teaspoon saffron
½ teaspoon sea salt

Put all ingredients in a pot. Bring to boil, lower heat and cook about 40 minutes.

## BULGAR MEXICANA

1 medium-sized onion, chopped
1 cup bulgar wheat
1 large stalk celery, thinly sliced
½ green or red bell pepper, seeded and sliced
1 teaspoon chili powder
¾ teaspoon ground cumin
2¼ cups vegetable stock
   salt & dash of cayenne pepper

Sauté onion and bulgar in a little olive oil, stirring occasionally, until onion is soft and bulgar is golden (7 to 8 min.) Stir in celery, bell pepper, chili powder, cumin, and cook for 2 minutes. Pour in stock and bring to a boil. Reduce heat to low; cover and simmer until all liquid is absorbed (about 20 min.). Season to taste with salt and cayenne. To serve, mound bulgar mixture on a platter or individual plates. At the table, offer condiments. Condiments: Prepare 1 cup each—shredded soy cheddar cheese, alfalfa sprouts, ⅓ cup each—sliced green onions, sunflower seeds, 2 tomatoes (diced), soy sour cream, salsa and chips.

## HOME-MADE SALSA

5 large tomatoes, chopped
½ large onion, chopped
1 - 2 jalapeno chili, take seeds out and mince
2 garlic cloves, minced
½ cup chopped cilantro
¼ teaspoon sea salt
   juice of ½ to 1 lime

Mix all ingredients together in a bowl. Ready to eat or you may chill it first.

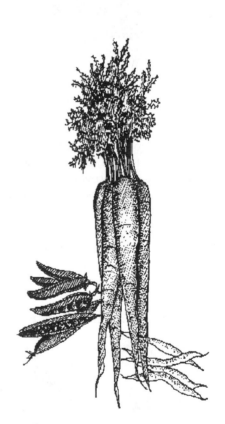

# Vegetables
# and Beans

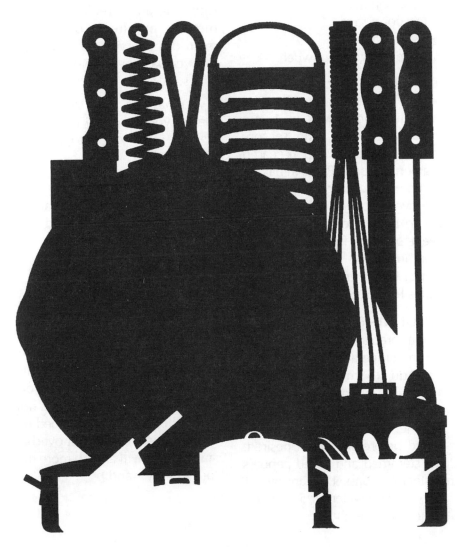

## STUFFED PEPPERS

8 large green peppers,
  stemmed and cored
1 onion, diced
½ cup celery, chopped
½ pound mushrooms, chopped
¼ cup water
2 cups tomato sauce (1 cup for
  topping)
3 cups cooked brown rice
1 teaspoon thyme
1 teaspoon sage
½ teaspoon basil
¼ teaspoon garlic powder

Cook onions, celery and mushrooms in water for about 15 minutes, until tender. Mix in 1 cup tomato sauce, rice, and seasonings. Pack mixture into prepared raw green peppers. Place in baking dish. Pour remaining 1 cup tomato sauce over peppers. Add 1½ cups water to bottom of baking dish to prevent peppers from drying out. Cover and bake at 375° for 45 minutes. Uncover and bake for 15 minutes longer. Serves 8.

### HELPFUL HINTS

May be prepared ahead of time. Keep in refrigerator until ready to bake. Add 15 minutes to baking time. As a variation, use 1 cup corn, fresh or frozen, in place of 1 cup rice. The green peppers may be steamed before stuffing, if desired. Place stemmed and cored peppers in a steaming basket. Steam over 1 inch of boiling water for 5 minutes. Stuff and bake as above.

## ZESTY TOMATO RELISH

2 large tomatoes, chopped*
2 zucchini, quartered and
  sliced
¼ teaspoon celery salt
1 small onion, minced
1 tablespoon lemon juice
½ teaspoon sea salt
5 dates, chopped
½ teaspoon sweet basil leaves

Combine all ingredients and simmer 30 minutes. For delicious main dish, serve over brown rice, or over pasta with toasted almond slices.

* you may use 1 can stewed tomatoes or you can use 1 can mexican stewed for a zippy topping over pasta.

## BAKED BEANS

6 cups cooked white beans
3 cups tomatoes, canned
¼ cup molasses
¼ cup honey
½ cup dates
2 cloves garlic, pressed
1 onion sliced

Blend dates with ½ cup water in a blender. Mix all remaining ingredients and salt to taste. Pour into a casserole dish. Put onion on top of beans. Bake at 400° for 1–2 hours or until beans have absorbed most of the moisture. (Do not overbake, since beans will absorb more moisture as they stand.)

## CHILI

1 cup onion, chopped
½ cup celery, diced
½ cup green pepper, diced
½ cup bulgur wheat
2 cups water
2 medium carrots, chopped
½ teaspoon cumin
1 tablespoon Grandma's Chili
  Seasoning
1 15-ounce can tomato sauce
1½ quarts tomatoes, fresh or
  canned
3 cups cooked kidney beans
½ teaspoon garlic powder
½ teaspoon sweet basil
  salt to taste

Sauté onion, celery and green peppers in ¼ cup water for 10 minutes. Blend carrots with 2 cups water and 2 cups tomatoes in a blender. Combine all ingredients and cook slowly for 20–30 minutes, stirring often. If it is too thick, add more water to obtain desired consistency. Serve with corn bread or other whole grain bread and a salad. For a big pot of chili, double the recipe.

## THREESOME BEANS

1 cup dried white beans
½ cup dried kidney beans
½ cup dried lima beans
4 tablespoons onion, chopped
2 tablespoons maple syrup
2 teaspoons salt

Combine all beans and soak 12 hours. Parboil a few minutes. Pour off water and rinse. Put onions in bottom of casserole dish, then add beans and remaining ingredients. Cover with boiling water at least 2 inches above beans. Bake 4 hours at 350°

## CECI BEANS
### (Garbanzo beans Italian Style)

1 15-ounce can garbanzo beans
2 tablespoons fresh parsley,
  minced
2 - 3 cloves garlic, minced
1 tablespoon olive oil
1 teaspoon lemon juice
  (optional)
  salt to taste

Mix all ingredients in a bowl. Best served chilled.

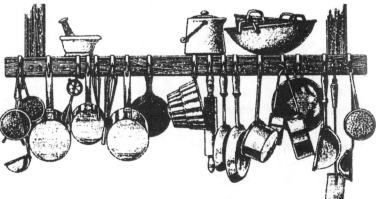

## VEGETABLE AND TOFU KEBABS

1 lb. firm tofu
1 small head broccoli cut into florets
1 yellow crook neck squash, cubed
1 zucchini, cut in rounds
1 large red onion, cut into crescents
1 red bell pepper, cut into large pieces
½ cup Bragg's Aminos
¼ cup lemon juice (or lime)
2 tablespoons sesame oil
1 tablespoon hot sesame oil
2 - 4 tablespoons honey
1 teaspoon garlic powder

Steam broccoli, bell peppers, and onion about 5 minutes. Add squashes and continue steaming another 5–7 minutes (just until crisp-tender. Do not overcook.)

Preheat oven to 375°. Cut tofu into 1 inch cubes and place on greased baking sheet. Squirt with some Bragg's. Bake about 20 minutes until light brown. Cool to room temperature.

In a large bowl, combine Bragg's, lemon juice, oils, honey, and garlic. Add tofu and vegetables; marinate 1–2 hours. Thread marinated tofu and vegetables onto skewers* and broil or grill for 5–7 minutes. Turn occasionally basting with remaining marinade. I serve these over a bed of rice. Serves 4.

*If using wooden skewers, soak them in water for at least 30 minutes before assembling kebabs. Soaking will prevent the skewers from burning while grilling.

## RICE STICKS WITH VEGETABLES

1 package rice sticks
1 bunch green onions, sliced
2 - 3 carrots, sliced
½ bunch broccoli, cut in florets (peel stem and slice)
½ cup peas
1 cup (or so) Bragg's Aminos
½ teaspoon garlic powder

Soak rice sticks in hot water. Sauté onions, carrots, and broccoli in water or a small amount of oil. Season with ¼ cup Bragg's and garlic powder. When vegetables are done, add peas. Transfer to a bowl. In the same pan, add 2 cups water and remaining ¾ cup of Bragg's. Bring to a boil and add rice sticks. Cook rice sticks until all moisture is absorbed, tossing frequently. If rice sticks are not done, add more water and Bragg's. When tender, toss with vegetables. (Add more garlic and Bragg's if more flavor is desired.)

# Potato Dishes

## BROWNED POTATOES

potatoes
oil
salt

Cook potatoes in skins, in salted water. Remove skins and place on baking pan brushed with oil. Sprinkle on salt. Brown in hot oven.

## SCALLOPED POTATOES

5 potatoes
1 onion, cut into rings
2 - 3 tablespoons whole wheat pastry flour
3 tablespoons oil
1/2 teaspoon salt
soy milk or Country Gravy (recipe pg. 70)

Scrub potatoes. Slice thinly, then place layers of potatoes and onion rings alternately in pan until pan is full. (Sprinkle flour and salt between layers). Cover with hot soy milk or diluted Country Gravy. Spread on a little oil. Bake at 425° until tender, about 1 hour.

## NEW POTATOES AND PEAS

7 potatoes, cooked whole
3/4 cup peas, steamed
Country Gravy (recipe pg. 70)
3 tablespoons parsley, chopped

Scrub potatoes and steam with jackets. Peel off thin skin, and cut into cubes. Mix with tenderized peas and Country Gravy. Add generous amount of parsley.

## CANDIED YAMS

5 yams, baked
1/2 - 3/4 cup honey or pure maple syrup
2 tablespoons oil

Peel and slice cold yams (after baking) into a baking dish. Alternate with honey or syrup, in layers. Sprinkle with oil. Bake until warmed through and slightly browned, or longer if you like them sticky.

## POTATOES AU GRATIN

6 - 8 potatoes, boiled and sliced
1 onion, chopped and sautéed
1 package Soya Kaas Cheddar Cheese
2 bricks firm tofu, crumbled
3/4 soy milk
2 tablespoons lemon juice
1/2 teaspoon garlic powder
1/2 teaspoon onion powder

Blend tofu, soy milk, lemon juice, garlic and onion powder in a blender. (Use enough soy milk to get a sour cream consistency.) Layer potatoes, sprinkle onion, tofu mixture, and then Soya Kaas Cheese. Continue layering until potatoes are used up. End with the cheese on top. You may need to add more soy milk on top to moisten. Bake at 350° for 30 minutes.

## SWEET POTATO CASSEROLE

4 cups sweet potatoes, mashed
½ cup hot soy milk
¼ cup honey
1 tablespoon oil
½ cup peanut butter
1 teaspoon salt

Add milk, oil and salt to sweet potatoes. Combine peanut butter and honey, and spread on the bottom of greased baking dish. Top with the sweet potato mixture. Bake 40 minutes at 375°. Garnish with fresh parsley.

## ITALIAN POTATOES

14 russet potatoes, cubed and
    boiled
2 red bell peppers, cut in strips
1 onion, cut in ½ rings
4 garlic cloves, minced
½ - ¾ cup fresh basil, chopped
2 cans Italian stewed tomatoes
1½ tablespoons Bragg's Aminos
1 teaspoon sea salt (or more
    Bragg's)
5 tablespoons soy parmesan
    cheese

Sauté garlic, onion, and bell pepper until tender. Add tomatoes, Bragg's, salt, and parmesan cheese. Simmer 10 minutes. Add potatoes and basil, simmer another 5–10 minutes. Remove to serving dish and sprinkle with more cheese.

## GOLDEN POTATOES ITALIAN STYLE

7 medium potatoes, small
    cubes, unpeeled
4 medium carrots, diced
1 large onion, chopped
4 tablespoons minced parsley
4 tablespoons oil
1½ cups water
    salt to taste (approximately
    1½ teaspoons) or chicken
    style seasoning
    pinch of saffron (optional)

Brown onion in oil. Add all remaining ingredients. Let cook over low flame—stirring occasionally until tender. Serve with tossed Italian salad.

## QUINOA POTATO CROQUETTES

2 cups potatoes, mashed with
    skins on
2 cups Quinoa, cooked
2 egg replacers
½ cup onion, chopped
½ teaspoon salt
½ teaspoon cumin
½ teaspoon oregano
¼ cup parsley, chopped

Combine all ingredients, mix well, form into 1" balls, and brown. Serve with Country Gravy.

## COUNTRY POTATOES

5 potatoes (red or russet)
½ teaspoon garlic powder
1½ teaspoon onion powder
¾ teaspoon sea salt
½ teaspoon paprika
   olive oil

Cut potatoes into big chunks. Boil or steam until tender, but not falling apart. Remove from the water. Heat a skillet with a little oil and add potatoes. Stir in seasonings. Brown 5–7 minutes.

## OVEN ROASTED POTATOES

10 potatoes (red or russet), cut into chunks or wedges
1 onion, cut into ½ rings
½ cup Bragg's Aminos
¼ cup olive oil
10 garlic cloves, leave whole with skin on
1 teaspoon garlic powder
1 teaspoon onion powder
1 teaspoon sea salt

Pour a little olive oil on the bottom of a casserole dish. Put in potato chunks, onion, and garlic. Cover with Bragg's, olive oil, garlic and onion powder, and salt. Bake at 350° until tender, checking and turning potatoes every so often, adding more Bragg's and seasonings if needed. Squeeze cooked garlic from skins to eat.

*Carrots and celery may be added to this also.

## POTATO SALAD

5 lbs. russet potatoes
½ small red onion, chopped
4 stalks celery, chopped
1 cup olives, sliced
¼ cup parsley, chopped
   Soy Mayonnaise (pg. 87)
2 tablespoons lemon juice
   sea salt to taste

Boil potatoes until tender. Rinse with cold water and cover with water. Place potatoes in refrigerator to cool. With a knife, peel off skins and cut into pieces. Add the rest of the ingredients just as you would regular potato salad. Add salt, if needed, to taste. Chill.

## COUNTRY STYLE GRAVY

3 cups water
½ cup cashews
2 tablespoons cornstarch
½ teaspoon sea salt*
2 teaspoons onion powder
½ teaspoon garlic powder
2 tablespoons Bragg's Liquid Aminos
1 tablespoon fresh parsley, chopped

Blend ½ cup water with cashews until smooth. Add the rest of the ingredients, except parsley. Pour into saucepan and stir while cooking until thickened.

* For chicken style gravy, omit salt and add 1–2 teaspoons ABCO Chicken Seasoning.

# Patties
# Meatballs & Breads

# Notes:

# NUT PATTIES

1½ cups ground Brazil nuts or
    pecans
1 cup soft bread crumbs
    (packed)
1 egg replacer
¼ cup onion, chopped fine
2 tablespoons parsley,
    chopped fine
1¼ teaspoon sea salt
1 cup soy milk

Mix ingredients together. Let stand 10 minutes. If mixture seems too thin, add some potato flour. Form into patties and bake at 350° for approximately 15–20 minutes. Then turn over and bake about 10–15 minutes more. Cover with gravy or Italian sauce.

**Helpful hint**
Tupperware hamburger press works great for making uniform patties.

# ZUCCHINI PATTIES

1 onion, diced
2 cups zucchini, grated
1 cup bread crumbs
½ ¾ cup flour
1½ 2 tablespoons ABCO Chicken
    Seasoning (to taste)
    salt (to taste)

Sauté onion in small amount of water. Mix all ingredients in a bowl and then form into patties. Brown in oven on both sides. Serve plain, or with gravy.

# MUSHROOM BURGERS

1 lb. finely chopped mushrooms
½ ground, toasted sunflower
    seeds
1 cup cooked lentils
1½ cups finely ground oatmeal
½ cup tomato-vegetable juice
¼ protein powder (optional)
⅓ chopped onion
⅓ chopped celery
1 teaspoon egg replacer
2 teaspoons Bragg's Aminos
2 teaspoons carob powder
    (optional)
    salt and cayenne to taste

Use a food processor to grind the ingredients, but be careful not to puree everything. Let this sit for 20 minutes. Preheat the oven to 350°. Form six 5-inch by ¾-inch patties and place on a lightly oiled cookie sheet. Bake for 15 minutes.

## LENTIL RICE PATTIES

2 cups cooked rice
1 cup cooked lentils
1 cup bread crumbs, packed
¼ cup flour
1 cup onion, chopped
2 egg replacer
1 teaspoon sea salt
½ teaspoon basil
2 cloves garlic, minced

Sauté onion and garlic. Add all the ingredients in a bowl, and mix. Form into patties. Bake at 350° until both sides are brown, or brown in a small amount of olive oil. These are good to make ahead of time and lay them in a casserole dish with some Italian sauce covering them. A tasty addition to this dish is to top with Cashew Pimiento Slicing Cheese (pg. 84).

## SUNFLOWER SEED PATTIES

1 cup raw wheat germ
4 cups raw sunflower seeds, ground
1 cup celery, diced
2 cloves garlic, diced
½ cup onion, minced
1 teaspoon sea salt
½ cup parsley, minced
1 tablespoon Italian seasoning
1 tablespoon olive oil
1 small can tomato paste

Mix all ingredients and form into patties. Bake at 350° for 10–20 minutes on each side. Serve these on a bun like a hamburger, or pour gravy over them.

## POTATO BURGERS

1 large potato, peeled and diced
1 cup cooked brown rice
¼ cup bread crumbs (almond rice bread, Italian or whole wheat)
3 tablespoons soy Parmesan cheese
½ onion, minced
1 - 2 teaspoons Bragg's Aminos
2 tablespoons parsley, chopped

Cook potato until tender. Combine remaining ingredients in a medium bowl. Drain potato and mash with a fork. Add the rest of the ingredients, and mix well. Form into patties. Brown on each side. Serve with Country Gravy.

## ITALIAN RICE BALLS

3 cups cooked brown rice
1 cup Soya Kaas Mozzarella
   Cheese
2 cups whole wheat bread
   crumbs (reserve 1 cup to
   roll balls in)
½ teaspoon basil
½ teaspoon oregano
6 teaspoons egg replacer
   mixed with
8 tablespoons water
2 tablespoons fresh parsley,
   chopped
1 teaspoon sea salt
1 teaspoon garlic powder

Mix all ingredients. (If rice is hot, you do not need egg replacer.) Form into balls. Roll in bread crumbs. Brown in a little olive oil, or bake in 350° oven until brown.

## TOFU MEATBALLS

1 large onion, finely chopped
1 large carrot, grated
1 green pepper, finely chopped
1½ teaspoon dried basil
   juice of 1 lemon
¼ cup tahini
3 cloves garlic, minced
¼ teaspoon dried oregano
1¼ cups bread crumbs
¾ cups walnuts, finely chopped
¼ cup fresh parsley, chopped
1½ tablespoons Bragg's Aminos
1 pound firm tofu

Sauté the vegetables and basil until tender, approximately 10 minutes. In a large bowl, add bread crumbs, walnuts and remaining ingredients. Mash the tofu and add it to the bowl, along with the sautéed vegetables. Stir well. (The mixture should be firm enough to form into 1½" balls. Bake on an oiled baking sheet for 20–30 minutes.

## CRACKED WHEAT / MILLET BREAD

2 cups hot water
¼ cup honey
2 tablespoons yeast

Whiz honey and hot water in blender. Add yeast. Whiz for a couple seconds, then let it stand for approximately 15 minutes. (I let it rise until it almost reaches the top of the blender.)

Pour into Bosch bowl, then add:
2 tablespoons sea salt
2 cups applesauce or
⅔ cup oil

Mix briefly, then add:
1½ cups unbleached white flour
1½ cups whole wheat flour

Mix on speed #1 until pasty, then stop. Then add:
5 cups hot water
2 cups whole wheat flour
2 cups unbleached white flour

Mix on #1 until flour is absorbed, then continue mixing while adding:
½ cup vital wheat gluten flour
½ cup millet
1 cup cracked wheat
½ cup wheat germ
1 cup baby oats
¾ cup oat bran

Then, 1 cup at a time, alternating, add:
about 3 cups whole wheat flour
about 2 cups unbleached white flour

Continue mixing until dough starts cleaning sides of bowl. Cover with lid and run for 10 minutes. Oil hands and counter top (don't use flour). Make loaves and put into warm oven or on oven door. Cover with thin, warm damp towel. Let it rise for 15–20 minutes. Turn oven to 350°, take off towel and bake for 45 minutes. Remove loaves from oven and brush tops lightly with oil. When almost cool place in plastic bags. This will help keep outside of bread soft.

## WALNUT "CHEESE" BALLS

1 cup walnuts, toasted and
finely chopped
3 cups soft whole wheat bread
crumbs
6 tablespoons dried onion
flakes
1 teaspoon salt
½ teaspoon garlic powder
3 tablespoons Do Pep
4 teaspoons dried parsley
¼ teaspoon marjoram
2 cups tofu, mashed

In a large bowl, combine seasoning and Do Pep. Stir in tofu, bread
crumbs and walnuts. Knead with
hands to mix thoroughly. Adjust
seasonings to taste. Roll into balls
about the size of walnut shells. (A
small amount of water may need to
be added if it seems dry, and the
balls don't hold together when
gently molded in the palms of your
hands. The mixture is right when it
is dry, but not gummy or sticky.)
Bake at 350° on sprayed cookie
sheet, uncovered, for 30 minutes.

## FALAFELS WITH TAHINI SAUCE

3 cups cooked or canned
garbanzo beans
¼ cup liquid from garbanzo
beans
¼ cup bread crumbs
1 small onion, finely chopped
2 garlic cloves, minced
4 tablespoons fresh parsley,
chopped
¼ cup sesame seeds
¼ tablespoon dried basil
¼ teaspoon dried oregano
1 teaspoon cumin
1 teaspoon chili powder
⅛ cup lemon juice
2¾ cup cracker crumbs, wheat
germ or bread crumbs

Combine garbanzo beans, liquid
and puree until smooth in blender.
Transfer to large bowl and add all
other ingredients except cracker
crumbs or wheat germ. Mix well.
Stir in enough cracker crumbs or
wheat germ until it holds together.
Roll mixture in 11 2-inch balls.
Place on a cookie sheet and bake
at 350° for 10–15 minutes per side
or until lightly browned with a
crispy, dry, cracked exterior. Be
careful not to let the falafels dry out
too much. The inside should be
moist. Put the following fixings
into pita bread with tahini sauce
(pg. 87): lettuce, tomato, onion,
cucumber and avocado. Option:
add fresh, chopped cilantro.

# Notes:

# Rice Dishes

# Notes:

## CALIFORNIA CASSEROLE

2 tablespoons olive oil
1 cup onion chopped
4 cups cooked rice
2 cups soy sour cream
1 cup tofu, crumbled
1 large bay leaf crumbled
½ teaspoon sea salt
    dash cayenne pepper
10 - 12 oz. Ortega whole green
    chilies (washed, drained
    and seeds removed)
2 cups grated soy cheddar
    cheese, and parsley

In a large skillet sauté onion in olive oil 5 min. Remove from heat and stir in rice, sour cream, tofu, bay leaf, and salt. In a 13x9 pan, spread ½ of the rice mixture, ½ of the soy cheese, lay chilies on top opened out flat. Repeat with rice and cheese. Sprinkle with parsley. Bake at 350° for 20–25 min.

## ORIENTAL RICE

4 cups cooked rice
3 - 4 tablespoons olive oil
1 2-ounce jar pimientos
½ cup bell pepper, chopped
½ cup silvered almonds
1 bunch green onions, sliced
¼ cup Bragg's Aminos
1 small can water chestnuts,
    sliced

Toss, then place in casserole dish and bake at 350° for 30–35 minutes.

## ROASTED GARLIC AND ORZO PILAF

(Orzo (OHR-zoh) looks like "big rice" but is actually an Italian baby pasta.)

8 - 12 large cloves garlic*
1 tablespoon olive oil
½ cup orzo
½ cup long grain rice
2 cups water mixed with
2 tablespoons ABCO Chicken
    Seasoning
¼ cup sliced green onions
1 tablespoon fresh chopped
    parsley

In a medium saucepan bring water and ABCO seasoning to a boil. Add rice. Peel and quarter garlic cloves. In a small skillet cook garlic in olive oil over medium heat until light brown. Add orzo and cook until light brown. (Do not let the garlic burn or it will become bitter.)

Stir orzo and garlic into rice. Continue cooking for 15–20 minutes or until orzo and rice are tender and broth is absorbed. Stir green onions and parsley into the pilaf.

*Resist the urge to cut down on the amount of garlic. As it cooks in the olive oil, the garlic softens and the flavor mellows.

## RISOTTO WITH MUSHROOMS

2 tablespoons olive oil
1 onion, chopped
4 cloves garlic, chopped
½ lb. fresh mushrooms, sliced
3 tablespoons. ABCO Chicken
   Seasoning
2 cups short grain brown rice
   (or arborio or pearl)
4½ cups water
1 teaspoon basil
3 tablespoons soy parmesan
   cheese
1½ - 2 cups tomato sauce or
   Italian sauce

In a saucepan, sauté onion, garlic, and mushrooms about 5 minutes. Add rice and stir 3–4 minutes. Pour in water, basil, and ABCO seasoning. Bring to a boil on high heat stirring often. Reduce heat. Simmer, uncovered, until rice is tender and most of the liquid is absorbed, about 25–30 minutes. Stir occasionally, and more often as mixture thickens. Remove from heat. Mix in soy parmesan cheese and tomato sauce. Bragg's Aminos may be added to this for a flavor enhancer.

## CONFETTI RICE

1 cup basmati or long grain
   brown rice
1 cup carrot, shredded
1 onion, finely chopped
1 teaspoon garlic, minced
3 tablespoons olive oil
2½ cups water
3 tablespoons ABCO Chicken
   Seasoning
½ cup parsley, chopped

Cook onion, garlic, and carrot for 5 minutes. Stir in rice and brown slightly. Add water, ABCO seasoning, and parsley, cover and cook 35–45 min.

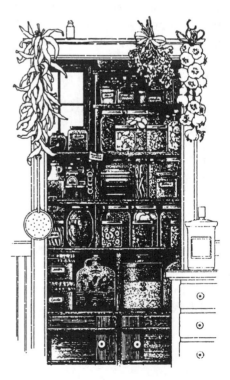

# Spreads

## PEANANZO SPREAD

(Nuteena-Like Sandwich Spread)
1 15-ounce can garbanzos, drained (save juice)
⅔ cup garbanzo juice
⅓ cup peanut butter
¼ teaspoon lemon juice
1½ tablespoons tomato paste
¼ teaspoon onion powder
⅔ cup olives, chopped

Blend all ingredients except olives and peanut butter. Add olives and peanut butter, and mix well in bowl. Makes 1½ cups spread. Delicious topped with sprouts and sweet onion on crackers, or used as sandwich filling.

## PIMIENTO DIP SPREAD

1 cup cashews
1 small jar pimientos
½ cup water (use part of liquid from pimientos)
2 small green onions (or onion powder)
½ teaspoon salt
lemon juice (optional)

Blend all ingredients well in blender for 2 minutes (until smooth). Stir in small amount of fresh lemon juice (to taste). Delicious on avocado, cucumbers, tomato and cabbage. Good spread for sandwiches or crackers.

## CASHEW PIMIENTO CHEESE

1 cup cashews
1 cup water
½ teaspoon salt
½ teaspoon garlic powder
1 4-ounce jar pimientos
¾ teaspoon onion powder
3 teaspoons lemon juice

Blend cashews and water until smooth. Put in a pan and cook, stirring constantly until it gets thick. (If this will be used in another cooked recipe such as lasagna do not cook in pan.) Return to blender and blend the rest of the ingredients.

*Add Ortega chilies for Nachos.

## PIMIENTO SLICING CHEESE

1 cup cold water
6 tablespoons Emes unflavored gelatin
1 cup boiling water
1½ cups cashews
3 tablespoons brewers yeast
2½ teaspoons sea salt
2 teaspoons onion powder
½ teaspoon garlic powder
2 tablespoons lemon juice
1 4-ounce jar pimientos
1 teaspoon paprika

Soak gelatin in cold water in blender. Add boiling water and whiz briefly to dissolve. Let stand to cool a little. Add cashews and whiz until smooth. Add remaining ingredients and whiz. Pour into container and refrigerate until firm. You can slice or grate this cheese. Ortega chilies are also very good in this recipe.

## PARMESAN CHEESE SUBSTITUTE

1 cup sesame seeds, lightly
   toasted
¼ cup yeast flakes
½ teaspoon onion powder
¼ teaspoon garlic powder
½ teaspoon salt

Put all ingredients in a dry lique-fier. Mill until seeds are milled, and ingredients are combined. Yields 1¼ cups. Great sprinkled on a fresh green salad.

## HOMMUS

2 cups cooked garbanzo beans*
1 - 2 cloves garlic
1 Tbls. parsley, chopped
1 - 2 Tbls. lemon juice (to taste)
   salt to taste

Blend garbanzos with barely enough bean broth to make blender turn. Add lemon juice and salt. Blend again. Stir in parsley. Dip with pita bread or serve as a spread on bread.
* Canned garbanzos may be used.

## BABA GHANOUSH

1 eggplant Bake at 350° for 45
   min. Cool for 45 min.
1 fresh lemon
2 cloves garlic, minced
1 tablespoon tahini
   salt to taste

Scoop inside of eggplant from the skin. Put in a bowl with other in-gredients. Mash with a potato masher. Spread on bread.

## CORN BUTTER

2 tablespoons Emes
   Unflavored Gelatin
¼ cup cold water
1 cup boiling water
1 cup corn meal mush*
1 rounded teaspoon salt
2 teaspoons lemon juice
1 teaspoon raw carrot, grated
¼ cup cashews

Soak gelatin in cold water for sev-eral minutes. (This can be done in a liquefier.) Pour the boiling water over gelatin, and whiz to dissolve. Add remaining ingredients and liq-uefy thoroughly, until smooth as cream. Pour into a shallow con-tainer, cover and refrigerate. Yields 2½ cups.

*For a smoother corn meal mush, soak corn meal overnight in its cooking water before cooking.

## 7 LAYER BEAN DIP

Refried beans (Rosarita
   Vegetarian or cook your
   own)
guacamole
Soy Sour Cream (pg. 86)
green onions, chopped
salsa
olives, chopped
cheese, Soya Kaas American
   cheddar and Jalepeno

Layer in a dish, getting a little smaller in diameter with each la-ger. Refrigerate Don't forget the chips for dipping!

## HONEY BUTTER

1 tablespoon Emes Unflavored
    Gelatin
¼ cup cold water
¾ cup boiling water
½ cup honey
½ cup cashews or almonds
½ cup corn meal mush*
1 teaspoon salt
1 tablespoon lemon juice

Soak gelatin in cold water for several minutes. (This can be done in a liquefier.) Pour the boiling water over gelatin, and whiz to dissolve. Add remaining ingredients and liquefy thoroughly, until smooth as cream. Pour into a shallow container, cover and refrigerate. Yields about 2 cups.

* For a smoother corn meal mush, soak corn meal overnight in its cooking water before cooking.

## SOY SOUR CREAM

8 ounces soft tofu
1 tablespoon honey
1 tablespoon lemon juice
¼ teaspoon salt

Put all ingredients in blender and liquefy.

## GARLIC BUTTER

1 cup water
1 cup warm corn meal mush*
½ cup cashews or almonds, raw
2 - 4 cloves garlic
1 tablespoon yeast flakes
1 tablespoon onion powder
2 teaspoons salt (if mush is
    unsalted)
4 teaspoons lemon juice)
½ cup sesame seeds
½ teaspoon marjoram
½ teaspoon dill weed

Liquefy all ingredients, except sesame seeds, marjoram and dill weed, until smooth (about 2 minutes). Briefly whiz in sesame seeds and herbs. Spread thickly on bread slices, and broil until crusty and beginning to brown. Yields 2½ cups.

* For a smoother corn meal mush, soak corn meal overnight in its cooking water before cooking.

## MUSTARD

¾ cup lemon juice
¼ cup soy flour
¼ cup soy flour
½ teaspoon sea salt
2 teaspoons turmeric

Place all ingredients in blender and whiz. Pour into a saucepan and heat until thick, stirring constantly.

Return to blender and add:
2 teaspoons garlic cloves
⅓ cup oil (slowly)

## MARGARINE A LA MILLET

1 tablespoon Emes Unflavored
    Kosher Gelatin
½ cup cold water
1 cup cooked HOT millet,
    packed
¼ cup cashews
½ tablespoon carrots, peeled
    and cooked
1 teaspoon salt

In a saucepan, bring 2 cups water to a boil. Add ½ cup millet and cover. Turn down to low heat and cook about 50 minutes. Be sure to keep the lid on tight, or millet will not be light and fluffy.

In another sauce pan, stir gelatin into cold water. Let stand for 5 minutes. Cook until gelatin is dissolved, and liquid is clear. Whiz cashews and ½ of the gelatin mixture until smooth. Add hot millet, carrots and salt. Whiz at low speed, increasing to high speed, until super smooth. Blend in the remaining ½ of the gelatin mix on low speed. Let stand a few minutes, so air bubbles can escape. Pour into containers and chill. Keeps 1 week. Yields 1½ cups.

## SOY DRESSING, MAYO, OR DIP

¾ cup water
½ cup Soyagen or Solait (solé)
¾ cup oil
1½ teaspoon onion powder
½ teaspoon garlic powder
1 teaspoon salt
½ teaspoon dill
½ teaspoon basil
3 tablespoons fresh parsley
    pinch thyme
2 teaspoons fructose
2 tablespoons lemon juice

*(for mayo delete dill, basil, parsley, thyme, and fructose)*

Put all ingredients in a blender (exept oil and lemon juice) and whiz. While blender is still going, slowly add oil *(for dressing, less oil may be used)*, and lemon juice. Refrigerate.

## 1000 ISLAND DRESSING

Make Soy Dressing and add:
¼ cup sweet relish (vinegar free)
¼ cup tomato paste

## TAHINI

1 cup sesame butter
1 cup water
2 tablespoons lemon juice
3 cloves garlic, minced
½ teaspoon salt

Stir all ingredients together in a bowl. Use in falafils or as a spread in sandwiches. May be used as a dressing—just thin down with more water.

## TOMATO DRESSING

Blend Thoroughly:
- ½ cup tomato puree
- ¼ cup olive oil
- ¼ cup lemon juice
- 2 cloves garlic
- ½ onion, chopped
- 1 tablespoon honey
- 1 teaspoon salt
- 1 teaspoon fructose

## HERBED ALMOND AND GARLIC SPREAD

- 1 cup bread, almond rice bread or whole wheat bread
- ½ cup blanched almonds
- ¼ cup olive oil
- ¼ cup fresh basil*, parsley, or cilantro
- 2 tablespoons minced garlic
- ¼ - ½ teaspoon salt
- ⅛ - ¼ cup water for a smooth spread

Put bread and garlic in food processor or blender. Place in bowl and sprinkle w/lemon juice. Place almonds in food processor and grind. Add lemon soaked bread crumbs and process well. Add oil, herb, and salt. Add water for a smooth spread.

*Our favorite is basil. It's great on whole wheat French bread served along with spaghetti or lasgna.

## CREAMY CUCUMBER DRESSING

Blend Thoroughly:
- ¾ cup Soy Sour Cream or Soy Mayonnaise (recipe pg. 87)
- ½ cucumber
- 2 tablespoons onion
- 1 - 2 tablespoons lemon juice to taste
- ½ teaspoon dill
- 1 clove garlic
- 1 tablespoon bell pepper, chopped
- 2 teaspoons fructose

## WILTED SPINACH SALAD DRESSING

- 1 red onion, slivered
- 2 cloves garlic, chopped
- 3 tablespoons olive oil

Sauté onion, garlic and olive oil. Pour over fresh spinach.

## CASHEW RANCH DRESSING

- 1 cup water
- 1 cup cashews
- 1 teaspoon basil
- 1 teaspoon onion powder
- ½ teaspoon garlic powder
- ½ teaspoon sea salt
- 1 teaspoon Bragg's Aminos
- 1 teaspoon fructose
- 3 tablespoons lemon juice

Blend cashews and water in blender until creamy. Add seasonings and lemon juice. Chill.

# Soups
# and Salads

# Notes:

## GARDEN FRESH MINESTRONE SOUP

3 medium-sized leeks
2 cloves garlic, minced
3 tablespoons olive oil
1 can kidney beans, with liquid
8 cups vegetable stock
6 cups prepared vegetables (to taste) (such as diced turnips and potatoes, sliced carrots, celery, zucchini, crookneck squash, green beans and peas)
2 cups cabbage, shredded spinach or chard
½ teaspoon dry basil
½ teaspoon oregano leaves
½ teaspoon dry rosemary
¼ cup tomato paste
½ cup elbow macaroni (optional)

In a 6-quart kettle, cook leeks and garlic in oil for 5 minutes. Add vegetable stock, kidney beans with their juice, vegetables, basil, oregano and rosemary. Simmer for 30 minutes. Stir in tomato paste, elbow macaroni (optional), and simmer until macaroni is tender. You may then add shredded cabbage, spinach or chard, and cook until it wilts. Salt to taste, and add more seasonings if needed.

## BORSCHT SOUP

4 quarts water
2 cups pinto beans, cooked
2 potatoes, cubed
2 carrots, sliced
3 stalks celery, chopped
½ bunch parsley, chopped
3 cloves garlic, chopped
1 large beet, sliced julienne
2 - 3 tablespoons ABCO Chicken Style Seasoning
1 bay leaf
1 cup peas
1 can stewed tomatoes
2½ cups cabbage, packed

Combine all ingredients except peas, tomatoes and cabbage. Bring to a boil, then cook over low heat 30 minutes. Add remaining ingredients and cook until done (approx. 10 minutes).

## SPLIT PEA SOUP

1 pound green split peas
8 cups water
1 onion, chopped
1 tablespoon dried parsley
2 bay leaves
3 teaspoons dried sweet basil
pinch of dill weed
pinch of cayenne pepper
1 teaspoon salt (to taste)

Combine all ingredients and bring to a boil. Then simmer 2–2½ hours, stirring often.

## LIMA BEAN SOUP

2 lbs lima beans cooked
4 potatoes, peeled and in
   chunks
4 lg. carrots, peeled and sliced
6 stalks celery, sliced
1 lg. onion, chopped
1 bell pepper, chopped
3 zucchini, chopped
2 cans stewed tomatoes
2 - 3 teaspoons basil
2 teaspoons sea salt
1½ teaspoons oregano

Sauté onion, garlic, parsley, potato, celery, carrot, and bell pepper
in a soup pot (about 5 minutes). In
a separate container mash some of
the beans (about ½) with a potato
masher. Add about 2 quarts water
to sautéd vegetables, and all of the
seasonings. Cook until vegetables
are almost done, then add zucchini, tomatoes, and all the beans
(mashed and unmashed). Continue
cooking until all vegetables are
tender.

## CORN CHOWDER

3½ quarts water
1½ quarts potatoes, peeled and
   diced
2 cups onion, chopped
2 cups celery, chopped
4½ quarts whole kernel corn
2 tablespoons onion powder
1 tablespoon garlic powder
3 tablespoons ABCO Chicken
   Seasoning
1 tablespoon sea salt

Combine ½ gallon water, 1½
quarts whole kernel corn, and all
other ingredients. Cook until tender. Then blend 1½ quarts water
with ¾ gallon corn in a blender.
Add to rest of mixture. Bring to a
boil.

## ZUCCHINI SOUP

6 - 8 small zucchini
4 - 5 bay leaves
½ medium onion, chopped
3 cloves garlic, chopped
1 - 3 tablespoons chicken
   seasoning
   Vegesal (to taste)

Combine zucchini, bay leaves, onion and garlic in saucepan, and
cover with water. Cook until tender. Remove bay leaves. Then
blend in a blender. Add remaining
ingredients and bring to a boil.

## RUSSIAN MILLET SOUP

1 cup millet
3 quarts water
2 stalks celery, chopped
2 potatoes, coarsely chopped
2 carrots, chopped
1 large onion, chopped
½ teaspoon salt
1 - 2 tablespoons ABCO
   Chicken Style seasoning
   small amount of tomato juice
   for color (optional)

Combine millet with water, and bring to a boil. Reduce heat and simmer 20 minutes. Add remaining ingredients and cook until tender.

## LENTIL STEW

1 pound lentils
6 cups water
3 potatoes, cut into chunks
3 carrots, sliced ¼ inch thick
3 stalks celery, sliced
2 bay leaves
1½ teaspoons basil
1 teaspoon garlic powder
1 teaspoon sea salt

Place all ingredients in a saucepan, and bring to a boil. Reduce heat and simmer until lentils and vegetables are done. If mixture gets too thick while cooking, add some water. This is very filling, especially over rice or barley.

## LENTIL RICE SOUP

1 pound lentils
½ cup brown rice
1 onion, chopped
1 bay leaf
1 teaspoon salt
½ teaspoon garlic powder

Put all ingredients in a small soup pot. Bring to a boil. Lower heat and cook 30–45 minutes.

Optional: celery, potatoes, or other vegetables may be added.

## CREAM OF POTATO SOUP

5 lbs. potatoes, cooked,
   pealed, cubed
2 onions, minced
4 stalks celery, chopped
2 carrots, shredded
1 - 1½ cups flour
6 - 8 cups Original Rice Dream
   Milk depending on desired
   thickness
2 tablespoons fresh parsley,
   minced
1 teaspoon dill
   salt to taste

Sauté onion, celery, carrot, and parsley until limp. Whisk in flour, then add about 2 cups milk, stirring constantly until thick. Continue stirring, adding the rest of the milk. Mixture should continue to thicken. Add potatoes, dill, and salt.

## NINE BEAN SOUP

¼ cup northern beans
¼ cup pinto beans
¼ cup large lima beans
¼ cup garbanzo beans
¼ cup kidney beans
¼ cup pink beans
¼ cup black beans
¼ cup navy beans
¼ cup small red beans
 1 large onion, chopped
   juice of 1 lemon
 3 cloves garlic, minced
 1 large can tomatoes
¼ - ½ teaspoon cayenne pepper
 2 tablespoons salt

Wash all beans and place in a large pot. Cover with water and 2 tablespoons salt. Soak overnight. (You may also use small amounts of lentils, split peas and barley.) Drain, add 2 quarts of water, bring to a boil, then simmer slowly about 2 hours. Add chopped onion, cayenne, lemon juice, garlic and canned tomatoes. Cook for another ½ hour. Add salt to taste. If soup gets a little thick add more water.

## CREAM OF VEGETABLE SOUP

In a big pot steam until tender:
 2 onions, chopped
 2 cups celery, sliced
 4 potatoes, peeled and
   chopped
 2 - 3 cups cauliflower, chopped
Add:
 4 cups shredded cabbage

When all vegetables are done remove steamer allowing veggies to remain in pot. It is OK to keep water left from steaming to remain in pot for the soup.

Add:
 1 - 2 cups peas.

In a blender whiz until smooth:
 1 cup water
 1 cup cashews

Add to vegetables plus enough water to make soup consistency:
 ¼ cup Bragg's Aminos
 1½ teaspoons garlic powder
   salt to taste

Heat until seasonings are blended but do not overcook.

*You can use the creamy base for other soups too: cream of broccoli, zucchini, corn, etc. Whiz some of the veggies in blender, after they have been steamed, with the cream base.

## ORIENTAL SALAD

8 cups Napa cabbage
1½ cups red cabbage
¾ cup green onion, sliced

Mix above ingredients in a bowl.
1 lb. firm tofu, cut into thin
strips or small cubes
½ cup Bragg's Aminos
2 tablespoons honey
1½ teaspoon onion powder
1 teaspoon garlic powder
½ pkg. rice sticks (check Chinese
section in grocery store)

Place tofu pieces on cookie sheet and season with the rest of the ingredients, tossing to cover tofu well. Bake for 20–30 minutes or until brown. Stirring occasionally. Let set to cool. Mix with cabbage.

Using a wok pan fill ⅓ with oil (canola or olive) heat on high. Place ⅓ of the rice sticks in oil. They should puff up quickly, as they do remove them promptly. Continue with the rest of the rice sticks. Toss with salad. Use Oriental Salad Dressing recipe.

## ORIENTAL SALAD DRESSING

⅓ cup toasted sesame oil
3 tablespoon Bragg's Aminos
3 teaspoons lemon juice
2 tablespoons water
2 teaspoons fructose

Mix all ingredients together. Pour over salad tossing gently. Top with ½ cup toasted slivered almonds and ⅓ cup toasted sesame seeds.

## FRESH CABBAGE SALAD

2 cups purple cabbage, grated
4 cups green cabbage, grated
1 cucumber, peeled and grated
¼ - ½ cup red onion, minced
1 - 2 carrots, shredded

Combine above ingredients, squeeze, and pour off liquid. Then stir in:
½ cup cilantro, chopped
2 tablespoons fresh parsley, chopped
½ teaspoon dill
½ teaspoon sea salt
½ cup lemon juice
½ cup brown rice syrup

Chill 1 hour or more to let flavors blend.

## TABOULI SALAD

Combine and let stand one hour:
1½ cups bulgar wheat
3 cups boiling water

Prepare the following:
1 tablespoon green pepper, finely chopped
¾ cup fresh parsley, chopped
3 fresh tomatoes, diced
¾ cup cucumber, diced
1½ bunches green onions, finely sliced
⅜ cup olive oil
½ - ¾ cup lemon juice
1 teaspoon sea salt or to taste

Mix all ingredients together and refrigerate. This recipe makes about 1½ quarts.

## COOL RICE SALAD

6 cups cooked brown rice, cooled
4 green onions , sliced
¾ cup cucumber, cut in small pieces
½ - ¾ cup peas, frozen, uncooked
3 tablespoons fresh parsley, finely minced
2 small tomatoes, diced
¾ cup celery, diced

Mix ingredients with soy mayonnaise (pg. 87) or the following dressing:
¼ cup lemon juice
½ olive oil
pinch of cayenne

Top salad with ½ cup toasted slivered almonds as a garnish.

## SALAD SONORA

1 cup lentils, sorted, washed, and drained
1 medium onion, peeled and chopped
2 cloves garlic, peeled and minced
1½ teaspoons chili powder
½ teaspoon ground cumin
2 cups water
1 cup frozen corn kernels
1 cup prepared salsa
1 4-ounce can chopped green chilies, drained
½ cup green bell pepper, chopped
½ cup sliced ripe olives, drained
½ cup chopped cilantro

In medium saucepan, combine lentils, onion, garlic, chili powder, cumin, and water. Bring to boil then reduce heat, cover and simmer about 15 minutes or just until lentils are barely tender. Drain, if necessary.

In large bowl, combine cooked lentils, corn, salsa, chilies, green pepper, olives, and cilantro. Cover and chill several hours or overnight to blend flavors. Serves 6.

NOTE: Salad can be served in taco shell, on thinly sliced fresh vegetables, or with tortilla chips.

* Black, kidney, pinto, or white beans may be used in place of lentils, if desired. Adjust water and time for cooking beans.

# Desserts

# Notes:

## POLYNESIAN BARS

1 cup millet flour
1 cup oatmeal, dry
⅔ cup applesauce
¾ cup unsweetened coconut
½ cup nuts, chopped

### CRUST

Mix all ingredients together with hands. This will make a crumb mixture. Press half of crust mixture into 9" x 12" baking pan.

### FILLING

4 cups dates, chopped
2 cups crushed pineapple, undrained
¾ cup water
1 teaspoon vanilla

Cook filling until thick and smooth. Add vanilla. Spread mixture on the crust to the edges of the pan, completely covering the crust. Add remaining crust, covering the filling, and pat down well. Bake at 350° for 30 minutes. Cool and cut into squares

## ALMOND JOY FUDGE

4 cups coconut, lightly toasted
¾ cup almonds, chopped
¾ cup date butter*
5 tablespoons honey
2 tablespoons flour
1 teaspoon vanilla
1½ - 2 cups carob chips
pinch of salt

*To make date butter, blend ½ cup dates with ¼ cup or more water in a blender.

Toast coconut at 250° until lightly brown. Mix date butter, honey, vanilla and salt together. Add coconut, almonds, and flour to mixture, and press into glass pan. Melt carob chips in double boiler. After they melt, add small amount of soy milk to make hot fudge consistency. Pour over coconut mixture. Chill.

## CAROB PEANUT BUTTER PIE

1½ cups water
2 cups carob chips
pinch of salt
½ cup soy milk powder
1 teaspoon vanilla
¾ cup smooth peanut butter

Blend above ingredients (except peanut butter) for about 2 minutes until smooth. Add peanut butter while still blending. Pour into pie shell (precooked) and freeze. Take out of freezer about 10 minutes before serving.

## PEANUT CANDY ENERGY NUGGETS

1½ cups flax seed, ground
1 cup sunflower seed, ground
1 cup almond butter or peanut butter
2 tablespoons wheat germ
½ cup walnuts, chopped
2 teaspoons vanilla
½ cup coconut
3 teaspoons carob powder honey or pure maple syrup

Mix all dry ingredients together in a bowl. Add nut butter. (You will have to use your fingers here.) Add enough sweetener to help it become stiff. Press into glass cooking dish. Refrigerate overnight. Cut into squares next morning.

## PECAN MAPLE LOGS

1 cup pecans, chopped fine
1 cup pecan butter
1 cup rice polish (grind to make finer)
½ cup pure maple syrup
1 cup dates, chopped pinch of sea salt

Mix all ingredients together except pecans. Roll into 9 ¾" x 3" logs. Roll in chopped pecans. Wrap in wax paper. Freeze or refrigerate.

## POPCORN BALLS

lots of popcorn
roasted peanuts (optional)
chunks of pecans
1 cup honey
1 cup carob chips
1 teaspoon vanilla

Melt honey and carob chips. Add vanilla, and pour over popcorn/nut mixture. Stir well to coat popcorn. Press into a casserole dish, muffin tin or anything else you have on hand. Ready to eat immediately.

## COOCOO FOR COCONUT

2 20-ounce cans crushed pineapple
1 12-ounce can pineapple juice concentrate or pineapple, orange, and banana juice
½ cup coconut
6 - 8 bananas
3 packages Nature's Warehouse Coconut Cookies
5 - 6 tablespoons cornstarch

Mix cornstarch with ½ of the pineapple juice. Set aside. Heat the rest of the juice, crushed pineapple and coconut until bubbly. Add cornstarch/juice mixture, and heat until thick, stirring constantly. Crumble 1½ packages of cookies on bottom of 9" x 13" baking dish. Next put a layer of banana slices. Pour pineapple mixture next, then another layer of bananas. Crumble rest of cookies on top. Press lightly, then chill in refrigerator.

## "HERSHEY'S" ALMOND BAR

4 cups barley malt-sweetened
  carob chips
½ cup almond butter or ¼ cup
  almond butter and ¼ cup
  peanut butter
½ cup roasted almonds

Melt almond butter in a double boiler or makeshift one. Add carob chips and melt thoroughly. Stir in almonds. Pour into a casserole dish. Put in refrigerator to harden. Cut or break into pieces.

## "REESE'S" FUDGE

4 cups carob chips
1 cup honey
1 cup peanut butter

In double boiler melt honey and peanut butter. Add carob chips. Melt over low heat until creamy. Pour into glass casserole. Chill and cut into squares.

## ALMOND CAROB BALLS

1½ cups almonds
¼ cup tahini
½ cup barley malt or rice syrup
1 tablespoon vanilla
2 tablespoon carob powder
1 teaspoon Bragg's Aminos

Dehydrate almonds one day to get a roasted flavor. Process almonds to a fine meal. Add remaining ingredients and process until well combined. Add enough carob to hold together. Shape into bars or balls. Roll in coconut and chill.

## PEANUT BUTTER COOKIES

1½ cups unbleached flour
½ teaspoon sea salt
½ cup canola oil
¾ cup peanut butter
¾ cup fructose
¼ cup date sugar
2 tablespoons soy milk

Cream peanut butter, sugars, milk and oil in a bowl. Add flour and salt. Roll into balls, then press down with a fork. Top with a couple of carob chips (optional). Bake at 350° for 10 minutes.

## OATMEAL COOKIES

5 cups oats (quick or regular)
2 cups flour
1 teaspoon salt
1 cup walnuts, chopped
  (optional)
¾ cup carob chips (optional) or
  raisins
½ cup coconut (optional)
½ cup water or soy milk
1 cup oil or 1 cup apple sauce
1 - 2 cups honey/maple syrup
  mixture
2 teaspoons vanilla
1 teaspoon maple flavoring,
  (opt.)

Mix all dry ingredients together. In a separate bowl, mix all wet ingredients. Add the mixtures together. Let sit 5–10 minutes. Drop free-form onto cookie sheet. Bake 15 minutes at 350°.

## OATMEAL CAROB CHIP COOKIES

1½ cups oats
½ cup whole wheat pastry flour
½ teaspoon salt
¼ cup oat bran
¾ cup walnuts
1 cup coconut
2 tablespoons vanilla
½ cup soy milk
½ cup honey
½ cup carob chips

Mix all dry ingredients together. Add honey, milk and vanilla. Make into rounded balls. Bake at 350° for 15 minutes.

## BANANA DATE COOKIES

3 bananas, mashed
1 cup dates, chopped
½ cup nuts, chopped
½ teaspoon vanilla
1 cup rolled oats
½ cup raisins
1 cup unsweetened coconut
1 cup dried papaya
½ teaspoon salt

Mash bananas. Stir in salt and vanilla. Add dates, nuts, raisins, coconut and papaya. Add oats last, and mix. Drop by tablespoon on Teflon or Pam sprayed cookie sheet. Bake at 350° for 25 minutes.

## TOFU LEMON PUDDING

1 cup water
½ cup boiling water
1 cup fresh lemon juice
1 cup cashews
1 cup (or less) honey
2 cups crumbled tofu
1 tablespoon agar powder
1 pre-baked pie shell

Soak agar powder in ½ cup boiling water for about 3 minutes. Blend with remaining ingredients in blender. Pour into pie shell and chill, or chill in dessert cups.

## MILLET PUDDING

2 cups HOT cooked millet
2 - 3 cups granola
½ cup pineapple juice
1 cup soy or rice milk
2 - 3 bananas
2 tablespoons maple syrup
½ teaspoon vanilla
½ teaspoon sea salt

Whiz all ingredients except granola and bananas in a blender until smooth. Sprinkle granola in bottom of casserole dish. Slice bananas and layer them on top of granola. Next, pour pudding mixture on top. Chill until thick. This is also good for breakfast.

## CASHEW RICE PUDDING

2½ cups brown rice, cooked
1½ cups soy milk
1 teaspoon vanilla
1 cup cashews
2 tablespoons honey
1 cup dates, chopped
¼ teaspoon lemon rind
¼ teaspoon orange rind
¼ teaspoon salt

Blend cashews in the soy milk until smooth. Mix with all other ingredients except rice. Fold into the rice. Bake at 350° for 30–40 minutes. DO NOT OVERBAKE! Serve plain or with Tofu Whipped Topping (pg. 107).

## CAROB PUDDING

8 cups soy or rice milk (Rice
    Dream Carob is the best)
2 teaspoons vanilla
½ cup pure maple syrup
2 cups carob chips
1 cup cornstarch*
2½ cups roasted walnuts,
    chopped (optional)

Bring 6 cups milk to a boil. Turn down to simmer. Dissolve cornstarch in remaining 2 cups milk, and add to heated milk. Cook until thick, stirring constantly. Stir in vanilla, syrup and carob chips, 2 cups walnuts (opt.). Stir until chips are melted. Pour into a casserole dish or dessert cups and cool in refrigerator. Sprinkle with remaining walnuts.

* For pie filling, use ½ more cornstarch.

## FRESH FRUIT PIE

5 - 7 cups cleaned and cut fruit
    (your choice peaches,
    strawberries)
½ cup pure maple syrup (to
    taste, depends on
    sweetness of fruit)
2 - 3 tablespoons cornstarch
1 prebaked pie shell

In a blender whiz 1 cup fruit, maple syrup and cornstarch. Pour into a pan. Cook on high heat until thickened, stirring constantly with a whisk. If not thick enough mix some cornstarch (not more than 1 tablespoon with some water). Stir into juice mixture. Pour over fruit that is in a bowl. Gently stir to coat fruit. Spoon into a pre-baked pie shell and chill until it sets up.

## CARAMEL CORN
## CLUSTERS

8 cups plain popped popcorn
6 cups Erewhon Aztec cereal
½ cup sunflower seeds
½ cup pumpkin seeds
1½ cups brown rice syrup

Heat syrup for 3 minutes. In a bowl, combine popcorn, cereal, and seeds. Pour syrup over mixture and stir until well blended. Spoon onto cookie sheet and put in oven for 7–10 minutes. Let cool completely and break into clusters. Store in an airtight container.

## BOYSENBERRY PIE

5 - 6 cups frozen boysenberries
½ - 1 cup pure maple syrup
(depending on tartness of
berries)
5 tablespoons cornstarch
prebaked pie shell (recipe,
pg. 107)

Thaw berries and drain juice into sauce pan. You should have about 1–1½ cups. Add syrup and cornstarch. Heat on high until thick, stirring constantly with a whisk. Pour over berries. If making an open face pie pour berries into pre-baked pie shell. The Soy Cream or Cream Cheese Topping is excellent on this. If a bottom and top crust is desired do not prebake bottom crust. Double the crust recipe. Divide into 2 balls, roll one ball and fit into pie dish. Poke holes in bottom, fill with berries. Roll remaining ball and place on top. Crimp edges and make slits so air can escape. Brush with a little soy milk and sprinkle with a little fructose. Bake 45–50 minutes until top crust is golden brown.

## CASHEW BANANA CREAM PIE

¾ cup cashews
2½ cups water
18 dates
3 bananas
1½ teaspoons vanilla
½ teaspoon salt
2 - 3 tablespoons cornstarch
1 pre-baked pie shell
½ - ¾ cup coconut

Blend cashews with 1 cup water until smooth. Add ½ cup water and all remaining ingredients except bananas. Blend until smooth. Add 1 more cup water and blend thoroughly. Cook over low heat until mixture thickens. Cool. Slice bananas and place 1 layer on baked pie crust. Cover with ½ of cooked filling. Add another layer of bananas, then add rest of filling. Sprinkle with more coconut, and chill.

## GOLDEN MACAROONS

Mix together:
1 cup grated carrots
½ cup crushed pineapple or
honey
¼ water
½ cup chopped dates
1 teaspoon almond extract

Add: 2 cups coconut
¼ cup whole wheat pastry flour
½ teaspoon sea salt

Let stand 10 minutes. Drop by rounded teaspoon on cookie sheet and bake at 325° for 30 minutes.

# "CHEESE" CAKE

## CRUST

3 cups granola
4 tablespoons soy milk
(enough to moisten, but not too wet)

Put granola in food processor and grind to desired texture. Add soy milk and mix thoroughly. Press into pie dish and bake 20 minutes at 350°.

## FILLING

2 containers Soyco Cream Cheese
1 container Soyco Sour Cream
¾ cup fructose or honey
3 tablespoons lemon juice
1 teaspoon vanilla
3 teaspoons egg replacer
4 tablespoons water
pinch of sea salt

Mix egg replacer with water and set aside. Beat cream cheese in food processor, or with an electric mixer until soft and creamy. Beat in fructose or honey. Add lemon juice, vanilla and salt. Continue mixing while adding egg replacer mixture and sour cream. Pour into pre-baked pie crust. Place in refrigerator and cool.

## TOPPING

½ container Soyco Sour Cream
⅛ cup honey
½ teaspoon vanilla

Beat all ingredients together, then spread onto cheese cake, or use berries that have been thickened and sweetened.

# YAM PIE

⅔ cup soy milk
½ cup pure maple syrup
1 cup cashews
2 teaspoons vanilla
½ teaspoon sea salt
3 teaspoons egg replacer
2 cups yams, cooked
⅛ cup light molasses or
½ - 1 tablespoon blackstrap
pinch cardamom

Blend soy milk, maple syrup and cashews until smooth. Add remaining ingredients and blend. Pour into pie shell and bake at 350° for about 40 minutes. Refrigerate. It will thicken more as it cools. Top with soy cream.

# APPLE TARTS

4 cups apples, peeled and shredded
½ cup water
1 6-ounce can apple juice concentrate
2½ tablespoons cornstarch

Blend cornstarch with a little water and set aside. Heat apple juice and ½ cup water in a saucepan. Add apples. Cover and simmer until tender. Stir in cornstarch mixture. Use Crumble Crust (recipe, pg. 106). Fill and bake 10 minutes at 350°.

## CRUMBLE CRUST

1½ cups dates
⅔ cup water
1½ cups Grape Nuts
1 cup quick oats
6 tablespoons almonds, chopped
¼ teaspoon sea salt

In a blender whiz dates and water to make a paste. In a bowl combine the rest of the ingredients. Add date mixture and stir thoroughly. (May need to use your hands.) Press into muffin tins for tarts. Bake at 375° for 10 minutes. Fill with apples. Reduce heat to 350° and bake another 10 minutes.

## COCONUT-DATE CRUST

(not your typical crust)
1 cup dates
¼ cup water
½ cup coconut
1 teaspoon lemon or orange rind
¾ cup walnuts, chopped

In a blender combine dates and water to make a very thick paste. Add coconut and lemon rind and blend. Spoon into a pie pan. Don't make crust too thick. Press walnuts all over and freeze. Fill with your favorite fruit filling.

## PEACH CRISP AND TOPPING

### FILLING

4½ cups fresh or canned unsweetened peaches
½ cup peach juice (if you are using fresh peaches put enough peaches in a blender to make ½ cup juice, and whiz)
¼ teaspoon vanilla
¼ cup dates
½ teaspoon coriander (optional)

In a blender whiz all ingredients except peaches. Stir mixture into peaches. Pour into casserole dish. Sprinkle generously with Crisp Topping (see recipe, below), or with Grape Nuts, or with granola. Bake at 350° until topping is golden brown (15 minutes or more).

### CRISP TOPPING

1½ cups quick oats
½ cup whole wheat pastry flour
¼ cup nuts, chopped
½ cup coconut
½ cup fresh squeezed orange juice or
2 tablespoons orange juice concentrate (mixed with ⅓ cup water)
¼ teaspoon salt
½ tablespoon vanilla)

Mix dry ingredients together. Add juice and vanilla. Mix well.

## PUMPKIN PIE

1 29-ounce can pumpkin
1½ cups soy or rice milk
⅔ cup cashews (toasted)
½ cup cornstarch
½ - ¾ cup pure maple syrup or
    honey
2 teaspoons vanilla
½ teaspoon coriander
½ teaspoon cardamom
½ teaspoon salt
½ teaspoon orange peel

Preheat oven 350°. Blend cashews and ½ cup milk until smooth. Add remaining milk and the rest of the ingredients. Blend until all ingredients are mixed thoroughly. Pour into pie shell and bake for 1 hour. Put in refrigerator to cool. Top with Tofu Whipped Topping.

## PIE CRUST

1 cup unbleached white flour
½ cup whole wheat pastry flour
¾ teaspoon sea salt
½ cup oil
⅓ cup milk *(soy or rice)*

Combine dry ingredients in a bowl. In a separate container mix wet ingredients. Stir the wet into the dry with a fork. Form into a ball. Roll between wax paper.

* This will make 1 crust. Double if a bottom and top crust is needed.

## TOFU WHIPPED TOPPING

2 cups tofu
4 teaspoons vanilla
½ cup honey
½ teaspoon salt
½ cup oil

Blend on high until smooth.

## CARROT CAKE

½ cup warm water
2 tablespoons yeast
2 teaspoons honey
½ cup soy milk
1½ cups carrots, finely grated
½ cup walnuts, chopped
1½ teaspoons orange rind
1½ teaspoons coriander
¼ cup coconut
2 - 2½ cups whole wheat
    pastry flour
½ cup oil
¾ cup honey
½ teaspoon salt
1 teaspoon vanilla
1 teaspoon maple flavoring
    pinch of anise (optional)

In a bowl, combine warm water, yeast and honey. Let stand until it bubbles, then add all remaining ingredients except whole wheat flour. Mix well, then stir in flour. Pour into oiled pan. Sprinkle coconut on top and let stand 10–15 minutes in a warm place. Preheat oven to 350° and bake for 45–60 minutes. This is a rich treat. Can be made into cupcakes baked in a muffin tin.

## GERMAN CAROB CAKE

1¼ cup whole wheat pastry flour

1¼ cup unbleached white flour

¾ cup toasted carob powder

3 teaspoons Ener G substitute baking powder

½ teaspoon sea salt

¼ cup oil

1 12-ounce can apple juice concentrate

½ cup pure maple syrup

2 tablespoons Roma mixed in ½ cup water

1 teaspoon vanilla

Mix all dry ingredients together in a bowl. In another container mix all wet ingredients. Pour wet ingredients into dry. Beat with an electric mixer until smooth, but do not over mix. Pour into greased and lightly floured 9" x 13" or two round cake pans. Bake at 350° for 35–40 minutes. Cool slightly before turning out onto a rack to cool completely.

Frost with Coconut-Pecan Frosting (see recipe, next column).

## COCONUT-PECAN FROSTING

1 cup pure maple syrup

½ cup water

1 cup coconut, toasted

1 cup pecans, chopped and toasted

½ teaspoon salt

2 tablespoons cornstarch mixed in

2 tablespoons water

In a saucepan heat syrup and water until bubbling. Add cornstarch mixture stirring constantly with a whisk until thick. Remove from heat and add the rest of the ingredients. Cool to room temperature before using.

## BANANA POPSICLES

bananas

melted carob chips*

peanuts, chopped

popsicle sticks

Peel ripe bananas and cut in half across width. Insert popsicle sticks. Coat bananas with melted carob chips and cover with chopped peanuts. Put in freezer to harden.

* Melt carob chips in a double boiler.

## FRESH STRAWBERRY ICE CREAM

1 tablespoon agar-agar flakes
1 cup cashews
3 cups water
1 tablespoon vanilla
2 cups fresh strawberries, chopped
¾ cup honey or pure maple syrup
⅓ cup oil
¼ teaspoon salt

Soak agar-agar flakes in 1 cup water. Boil 1 minute, cool 1 minute, then add cashews, and blend until smooth. Add remaining water, vanilla and 1 cup chopped strawberries, liquefy. Add honey and salt. Blend, adding oil slowly while blending. Continue blending for 1 more minute. Add remaining chopped strawberries. Pour into ice cream maker and process. This is the best way, but if you don't have an ice cream maker, freeze in a bowl or tray. Serve before it gets hard.

## BANANA HONEY SOYMILK ICE CREAM

1 gal. (16 cups) rich soymilk
6 bananas, frozen
1⅓ cups light vegetable oil
2 - 2¼ cups honey
2 tablespoons slippery elm, guar gum, or carrageenan
½ teaspoon vanilla extract
⅔ cup powdered lecithin or ⅛ cup liquid lecithin
½ teaspoon salt
⅛ cup agar
1 cup water
1½ cups chopped walnuts

Combine in large blender: 4 cups soymilk, 6 frozen bananas, ¾ cup oil, and next five ingredients; blend until smooth. Pour into large pot, together with 8 more cups of soymilk. Combine agar and water in a sauce pan, bring to a boil, and simmer for two minutes. Pour into blender together with remaining 4 cups of soymilk and oil. Blend until smooth, then pour into pot. Stir in chopped walnuts, then transfer mixture to ice cream freezer and freeze. Yield: 2 gallons

## BANANA CREAM PIE

10 whole graham crackers,
    ground into fine crumbs
¼ cup fructose
6 tablespoons melted soy
    margarine
¾ cup fructose or turbinado
    sugar
5 tablespoons cornstarch
1½ cups regular soy milk (or rice)
½ teaspoon salt
2 tablespoons soy margarine
½ pound firm tofu
4 large bananas
⅓ cup coarsely chopped,
    roasted almonds

Combine the cracker crumbs, ¼ cup fructose, and soy margarine until completely mixed. Press into the bottom and along the sides of a 9½ inch pie pan. Bake at 350° until lightly toasted, about 20 minutes. Let cool.

Combine the sugar and cornstarch, then add the soy milk, (or rice) vanilla, and salt. Whisk until well blended. Add the soy margarine and place in a double boiler. Cook over a medium heat, stirring frequently, until very thick. Refrigerate until chilled, then blend in a food processor with the tofu until smooth and creamy.

Slice the bananas over the cooled crust. Pour the custard on top. Sprinkle with the toasted nuts, and refrigerate until firm, at least an hour.

## PINEAPPLE PIE

2 cups Rice Dream Milk
1 cup cashews, blanched
⅓ cup + cornstarch
⅔ cup pure maple syrup
2 teaspoons vanilla
½ teaspoon salt
1 large can crushed pineapple
    (juice also)

Whiz cashews and 1 cup milk in blender until creamy. Then add the rest of milk and remaining ingredients. If you prefer pineapple pieces, do not add to blender. Heat until thickened, stirring constantly with a whisk. Pour into pie shell.

Crust for Pineapple Pie:
1½ cup toasted coconut
2 cups almonds or pecans,
    ground
⅓ cup maple syrup

Combine ingredients and press into a 10" pie plate and chill.

# References for
# Living Well

# Notes:

## READ THIS BEFORE YOU DRINK YOUR NEXT CUP OF COFFEE OR TEA

### HEART ATTACK

An extensive study by Dr. Hershel Jick of the Boston University Medical Center indicates that those people who drink 1 to 5 cups of coffee per day are likely to have a 60% greater risk of heart attacks. Those people drinking 6 or more cups per day appear to have a 120% greater risk than do those who abstain.

The American Physical Fitness Research Institute reports: "A positive correlation has been found between coffee intake and blood cholesterol levels in coronary patients."

### CANCER

According to scientists from the Department of Epidemiology, and Kresge Center of Environmental Health at Harvard University, "About 25% of the bladder cancer in men, and about 49% of the bladder cancer in women could be due to coffee drinking."

### BIRTH DEFECTS

National syndicated columnist Jack Anderson reported that "A University of Illinois team found that too much caffeine could cause birth complications. Of the 16 pregnant women who drank 6 to 8 cups of coffee per day, all but one had nasty consequences." "In addition," he wrote, "another team of scientists, this one at the University of Washington, has come up with corroborative findings."

### CAFFEINE IS IN COFFEE AND TEA

Coffee contains 100 to 150 milligrams of caffeine per cup, and commercial tea has about 90 milligrams per cup. Besides caffeine, tea also contains tannic acid, which is used in the hardening of leather.

### DECAFFEINATED COFFEE IS NOT THE ANSWER

Methylene chloride is the substance used to decaffeinate coffee. It introduces the same carbon-to-chloride bond into the body that is characteristic of many toxic insecticides.

### TRY ONE OF THESE COFFEE SUBSTITUTES

Postum
Pero
Breakfast Cup
Cafix
Roma *(our personal favorite)*
Nature's Sunshine Herbal
   Beverage
(ingredients: roasted barley, rye, malt, chicory and herbal flavorings)
Provita's Herbal Cafe
(ingredients: roasted barley, rye, malt, chicory and freeze dried beet root)

# ORIGINAL BIBLE DIET
# BEST FOR MAN TODAY

"Behold I have given YOU every herb bearing seed, which is upon the face of all the earth, and every tree, in the which is the fruit of a tree yielding seed; to YOU it shall be for meat." Genesis 1:29

The following explanation of Genesis 1:29 is given according to FOODS as we know them today:

"BEHOLD I HAVE GIVEN YOU EVERY HERB BEARING SEED...." (A seed plant which does not develop woody persistent tissue).

- GRAINS — wheat, corn, rye, barley, rice, millet, oats, buckwheat, etc.
- SEEDS — sunflower, sesame, flax, pumpkin, etc.
- LEGUMES — soybeans, lentils, peas, peanuts, other beans, etc.
- SUCCULENT FOODS CONTAINING SEED — eggplant, okra, bell pepper, squash, green beans, pumpkins, cucumbers, tomatoes, melons, etc.

".... and EVERY TREE, in the which is THE FRUIT OF A TREE YIELDING SEED...." (A woody perennial plant, shrub or bush).

- FRUITS — citrus fruits, sub-acid fruits, sweet fruits, palm fruits, neutral fruits.
- NUTS — almonds, pecans, cashews, Brazil, walnuts, chestnuts, filberts, macadamia, acorns, pine nuts, etc.

".... to YOU it shall be for MEAT." Genesis 1:29.

---

Ten Talents, Dr. Frank J. Hurd, D.C., and Rosalie Hurd, B.S.

# THE GREEN HERBS
# ORIGINALLY ANIMALS' FOOD

"And to every BEAST of the earth, and to every FOWL of the air, and to every THING that creepeth upon the earth…. I have given every GREEN HERB FOR MEAT: and it was so." Genesis 1:30

After man sinned, he was driven out of the Garden of Eden, and no longer had access to the wonderful Tree of Life. Man had to gain his livelihood by tilling the earth, and the "herb of the field" (originally food for the animals) was added to his diet.

"And unto Adam He said, 'Because thou has harkened unto the voice of thy wife…cursed is the ground for thy sake…and thou SHALT EAT the HERB of the field." Genesis 3:17, 18.

**VEGETABLES (HERBS)**
- Leafy: beet greens, Brussels sprouts, cabbage, collard, mustard greens, turnip greens, endive, kale, lettuce, chard, spinach, parsley, watercress, etc.
- Flower: globe artichoke, broccoli, cauliflower
- Root: carrots, beets, potatoes, turnips, etc.

Although vegetables (green herbs) were not part of the ORIGINAL DIET given to man, they were added to man's diet after he sinned, and are a part of his diet today.

"Grains, fruits, nuts and vegetables constitute the diet chosen for us by our Creator." *Counsels on Diet and Foods,* pg. 81—E.G. White

Ten Talents, Dr. Frank J. Hurd, D.C., and Rosalie Hurd, B.S.

# Laws
# of
# Health

# 8 LAWS OF HEALTH: AS DIVINE AS THE 10 COMMANDMENTS

"God has formed laws to govern every part of our constitutions, and these laws which He has placed in our being are divine, and <u>for every transgression there is a fixed penalty</u>, which sooner or later must be realized."

*Healthful Living pg. 20*

# G.O.D.S.  P.L.A.N.

- **G**odly Trust
- **O**pen Air
- **D**aily Exercise
- **S**unshine

- **P**roper Rest
- **L**ots of Water
- **A**lways Temperate
- **N**utrition

# DISEASE NEVER COMES WITHOUT A CAUSE!

"God has endowed us with a certain amount of vital force. He has also formed us with organs suited to maintain the various functions of life, and He designs that these organs shall work together in harmony. If we carefully preserve the life force, and keep the delicate mechanism of the body in order, the result is health; but if the vital force is too rapidly exhausted, the nervous system borrows power for present use from its resources of strength, and when one organ is injured, all are affected. Nature bears much abuse without apparent resistance; she then arouses and makes a determined effort to remove the effects of the ill-treatment she has suffered. Her effort to correct these conditions is often manifest in fever and various other forms of sickness." *Ministry of Healing, pg. 234, 235*

# The Laws of God

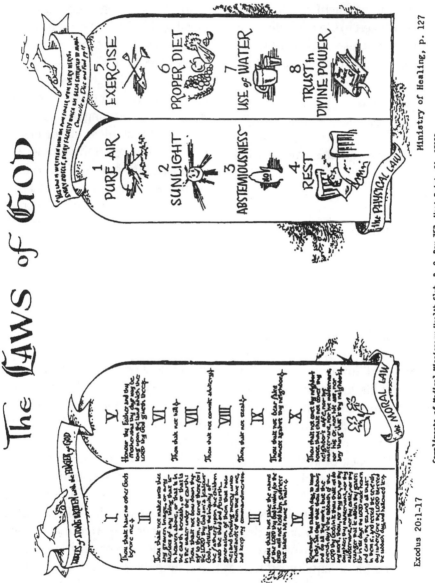

This Law is Written with the Finger upon every nerve, Every Muscle, Every Faculty which has been Entrusted to man.
_Counsels on Diet and Foods, p. 17_

**The PHYSICAL LAW**

1. PURE AIR
2. SUNLIGHT
3. ABSTEMIOUSNESS
4. REST
5. EXERCISE
6. PROPER DIET
7. USE of WATER
8. TRUST in DIVINE POWER

Ministry of Healing, p. 127

Ten Commandments Written with the FINGER of GOD

**The MORAL LAW**

I. Thou shalt have no other Gods before me.

II. Thou shalt not make unto thee any graven image...

III. Thou shalt not take the name of the LORD thy God in vain...

IV. Remember the sabbath day to keep it holy...

V. Honour thy Father and thy Mother...

VI. Thou shalt not kill.

VII. Thou shalt not commit adultery.

VIII. Thou shalt not steal.

IX. Thou shalt not bear false witness against thy neighbour.

X. Thou shalt not covet...

Exodus 20:1-17

Compliments of Medical Missionary Health Club, P. O. Box 752, West Point, CA 95255.
Printed and published by Harvest Time Ministries, P. O. Box 84, Rancho Cordova, CA 95670.

# HEALTH PRINCIPLES
# THE LAWS OF HEALTH

"Pure air, sunlight, abstemiousness, rest, exercise, proper diet, the use of water, trust in Divine power—these are the true remedies." MH, pg. 127

## 1—FRESH AIR

"And God called the firmament Heaven." Gen. 1:8

The most essential element to sustain life is oxygen.

- Without food you will die in a few weeks.
- Without water you will die in a few days.
- Without air you will die in a few minutes.
- Blood and cells are dependent upon oxygen.

Fresh air invigorates the vital organs and aids the system in ridding accumulated impurities. Fresh air also brings life to the skin and has a decided influence on the mind. Fresh air contains negative ions which help the immune system fight disease. The lack of fresh air causes specific problems such as fevers, colds, and lung diseases.

"The stomach, liver, lungs and brain are suffering for want of deep, full inspirations of air which would electrify the blood and impart to it a bright, lively color, and which alone can keep it pure, and give tone and vigor to every part of the living machinery." 2T, pg. 67–68

In the morning, step outside and breather deeply, then expel all the air in your lungs. Repeat this about 3 or 4 times. Have fresh air ventilating in your home day and night. Exercise in the open air will promote good circulation. Air is the free blessing of Heaven.

"In the matchless gift of His Son, God has encircled the whole world with an atmosphere of grace as real as the air which circulates around the globe. All who choose to breathe this life-giving atmosphere will live and grow up to the stature of men and women in Christ Jesus." Steps to Christ, pg. 68

## 2—SUNSHINE

"And God made two great lights; the greater light to rule the day." Gen. 1:16

Every living thing in our world is dependent on sunlight. Without sunlight, nothing would live. The following discoveries show the benefits derived from the sun: It lowers blood sugar and blood pressure; it lowers cholesterol by converting it to vitamin D; it utilizes calcium and phosphorus; it increases red blood cells; it increases white blood cells; it strengthens the immune system; it calms the nerves and increases adrenaline; it destroys germs on the skin; it reverses jaundice; it increases circulation; and it helps eliminate pesticides and other chemicals from the system.[1]

"Pure air, good water, sunshine, the beautiful surroundings of nature...these are God's means for restoring the sick to health." 7T, pg. 85

Start the day with exposing your face and body to the sun for 10 to 15 minutes. Gradually increase your time to 30 to 45 minutes daily. DO NOT GET A SUNBURN. The best time for sunbathing is between 9:00 and 10:00 AM and between 4:30 and 5:30 PM.

"As the flower turns to the sun, that the bright beams may aid in perfecting its beauty and symmetry, so should we turn to the Son of Righteousness, that Heaven's light may shine upon us, that our character may be developed into the likeness of Christ." SC, pg. 68

## 3—ABSTEMIOUSNESS
"Of the ground made the Lord to grow every tree that is good for food." Gen. 2:9

Abstemiousness means temperance. True temperance teaches us to dispense entirely with everything harmful and to use judiciously that which is healthful.

Avoid anything that is harmful to your body. This includes liquor, drugs, tobacco, overeating, eating between meals, sugar laden foods, strong condiments and spices, all caffeinated foods (chocolates and some sodas contain caffeine, as do coffee and tea), large combinations of foods, grease and fat, excess salt, and animal foods. "Indulgence in eating too frequently, and in too large quantities, overtaxes the diges-tive organs, and produces a feverish state of the system. The blood becomes impure, and then diseases of various kinds occur." RH 9-5-1899

Temperance is a Bible doctrine.
- It is a fruit of the Spirit. Rom. 5:23
- It is a sound doctrine. Titus 2:1
- It is part of the process of sanctification. 2 Peter 1:6
- Paul included it in his testimony to Felix. Acts 24:25
- Paul taught that a man who strives for the mastery is temperate in all things. I Cor. 9:25

"Abstemiousness in diet and control of the passions, will preserve the intellect and give mental and moral vigor, enabling men to bring all their propensities under the control of the higher powers, and to discern between right and wrong, the sacred and the common." 3T pg. 491

"I beseech you therefore, brethren, by the mercies of God, that ye present your bodies a living sacrifice, holy, acceptable unto God, which is your reasonable service. And be not conformed to this world: but be ye transformed by the renewing of your mind, that ye may prove what is that good, and acceptable, and perfect, will of God." Rom. 12: 1,2

## 4—REST
"He rested the seventh day from all His work which He had made." Gen.2:2

- The greatest remedy for being tired is SLEEP.
- The body requires plenty of rest to heal.

- Sleep is the greatest rejuvenator; it restores strength to muscles, nerves, and brain.
- During sleep the body repairs, reenergizes, and prepares for renewed activity.
- One hour of sleep before midnight is equal to 2 hours of sleep after midnight

During a day of work and activity, toxins build up in our system which cannot immediately be thrown off. These toxins produce fatigue—that well-known weariness at the end of the day. Sleep gives the body time to expel wastes and to make repairs.

"The stomach, when we lie down to rest, should have its work done, that it may enjoy rest, as well as other portions of the body. The work of digestion should not be carried on through any period of the sleeping hours." Healthful Living, pg. 84

Rest is not synonymous with sleep. Four types of rest are:

- Physical Rest—sitting, lying down, or relaxing. Not eating late at night or before bed.
- Sensory Rest—quietness and refraining from using the eyes.
- Emotional Rest—by withdrawing from the ups and downs caused by personal interaction.
- Mental Rest—which is obtained by detaching the mind from all intellectual demands or activity.

Your Prescription: First, get the sleep your body needs; 8 hours a day and several hours before midnight. Second, do not neglect that important rest we need such as: taking morning walks, sitting in a Jacuzzi, or by a mountain side, looking at a forest or lake, going to the ocean, or reading the scriptures.

"A life in Christ is a life of restfulness. There may be no ecstasy of feeling, but there should be an abiding, peaceful trust. Your hope is not in yourself, it is in Christ. Your weakness is united to His strength, your ignorance to His wisdom, your frailty to His enduring might.... Let the mind dwell upon His love, upon the beauty, the perfection of His character." SC, pg. 70

## 5—EXERCISE

"God put him in the garden of Eden to dress it and to keep it." Gen. 1:15

"God designed that the living machinery should be in daily activity. For in this activity or motion is its preserving power.... The more we exercise, the better will be the circulation of the blood." HL, pg. 131–132

"There is no exercise that can take the place of walking. By it the circulation of the blood is greatly improved. Walking, in all cases where it is possible, is the best remedy for the diseased bodies, because in this, all of the organs of the body are brought into use." 3T, pg. 78

"Moderate exercise every day will impart strength to the muscles, which without exercise become flabby and enfeebled." 2T, pg. 533

"Exercise will aid in the work of digestion. Take a walk after a meal;

but no violent exercise after a full meal." 2T, pg. 530

"Morning exercise, walking in the free, invigorating air of heaven, or cultivating flowers, small fruits, and vegetables is the surest safeguard against colds, coughs, congestion of the brain, inflammation of the liver, the kidneys, and the lungs, and a hundred other diseases." HL, pg. 176

Studies are finding that exercise is an important factor in the fight against cancer.

"If physical exercise were combined with mental exertion, the blood would be quickened in its circulation, the action of the heart would be more perfect, impure matter would be thrown off, and new life and vigor would be experienced in every part of the body." Counsels on Health, pg. 572

"Those who thus exercise the Christian graces will grow and will become strong to work for God. They will have clear spiritual perceptions, a steady growing faith, and an increased power in prayer.... Strength comes by exercise. Activity is the very condition of life. Those who endeavor to maintain a Christian life by passively accepting the blessings that come through the means of grace, and doing nothing for Christ, are simply trying to live by eating without working.... A man who would refuse to exercise his limbs would soon lose all power to use them. Thus the Christian who will not exercise his God-given pow-

ers, not only fails to grow up into Christ, but he loses the strength that he already had." SC, pg. 80

## 6—WATER
"And a river went out of Eden and watered the garden." Gen. 2:10

The body requires water constantly. Most of this water is recycled within the body itself. However, it must have a replacement of eight glasses of water per day. Cleansing of waste material is a daily task for the body, not only from its own wastes, but from the constant bombardment of germs and viruses, and in today's society, from chemicals and drugs. If the body is not thoroughly cleansed, it is forced to break down. "Water is the best liquid possible to cleanse the tissues.... Drink some, a little time before or after a meal." HL, pg. 226

Frequent bathing is very beneficial, especially at night before retiring or upon arising in the morning. "The bath soothes the nerves. It promotes general perspiration, quickens the circulation, overcomes obstructions in the system, and acts beneficially on the kidneys and the urinary organs. Bathing helps the bowels, stomach, and liver, giving energy and new life to each. It also promotes digestion and instead of the system being weakened, it is strengthened...and a more easy and regular flow of the blood through all the blood vessels is obtained." CH, pg. 104

123

"Impurities are constantly and imperceptibly passing from the body, through the pores, and if the surface of the skin is not kept in a healthy condition, the system is burdened with impure matter. If the garments worn are not frequently cleansed.... the pores of the skin absorb again the waste matter thrown off. The impurities of the body are taken back into the blood and forced upon the internal organs." HL, pg. 143

Food should not be washed down, and no drink is needed with meals. Eat slowly and allow the saliva to mingle with the food. The more liquid there is taken into the stomach with the meals, the more difficult it is for the food to digest, for the liquid must first be absorbed.

Many make a mistake in drinking cold water with their meals. Taken with meals, water diminishes the flow of the salivary glands, and the colder the water, the greater the injury to the stomach. The best time to drink your water is a half hour before or an hour after your meals. A couple large glasses of hot water first thing in the morning will assist your bowels in elimination.

Other benefits of water are hydrotherapy, hot and cold fomentations, enemas, etc.

"God is the source of life and light and joy to the universe. Like rays of light from the sun, like the streams of living water bursting from a living spring, blessings flow out from Him to all His creatures. And wherever the life of God is in the hearts of men, it will flow out to others in love and blessing." SC pg. 77

## 7—NUTRITION

"And God said, 'Behold, I have given you every herb bearing seed...and every tree in the which is the fruit of a tree yielding seed; to you it shall be for meat.' "

Gen. 1:29

Proper nutrition is vital to good health. Food that is devitalized cannot supply the vitamins and minerals it lacks. Therefore, it is of utmost importance that we choose wisely the food that goes on our table. Vegetables and fruits should be taking up the greater proportion of our meals, with whole grains, beans, legumes, and seeds. Nuts can be included in small amounts. From our food, we will obtain all the elements essential for good health: vitamins, minerals, water, carbohydrates, protein, fats, and fiber.

Foods should be prepared with simplicity and variation, perhaps only three or four dishes at a meal, and properly cooked. Food should be carefully chosen and prepared with intelligence and skill. Avoid the use of grease in foods. Lard, butter, and hydrogenated vegetable fats may be classified as grease. If using oil, use natural oils sparingly, such as olive, flax, or canola, and keep refrigerated.

Avoid sugar. It is not good for the stomach, because it causes fermentation. Milk and sugar clog the system, irritate the digestive organs, and affect the brain. Sugar, when largely used, is more injurious than meat.

Eat raw vegetable salads or raw fruits before the main course. This will stimulate and assist digestion, and help avoid overeating of cooked foods. Fruits and vegetables should not be eaten at the same meal. Eat fruits at one meal and vegetables at another.

Eat sparingly—for strength and not for drunkenness. The benefit you derive from your food does not depend so much upon the amount eaten, as upon its proper combination and thorough digestion. Neither does gratification of taste depend so much upon the amount of food swallowed as upon the length of time it remains in the mouth. Overeating clogs the machinery and weakens the moral power to resist other passions.

Eat at regular intervals, allowing 5–6 hours to elapse between meals. Do not eat a morsel of food between meals. When hungry between meals, drink a large glass of cool water. Do not eat before going to bed. The stomach must not be constantly at work, but have periods of rest.

Take time to eat and enjoy mealtimes. Avoid eating compulsively or when emotionally upset, in pain, or overtired.

Eat a substantial breakfast. In the morning, after a good night's rest, the stomach is far better able to digest a hearty meal than at other meals of the day. The practice of eating a little or no breakfast and a heavy supper may be conducive to putting on unwanted pounds.

Two meals a day are better than three, but if a third meal is eaten at all, it should be light, and eaten several hours before going to bed. Example: two meals—8AM and 3PM or three meals—6AM, 12PM, and 6PM.

In the grains, fruits, vegetables, nuts, and seeds are found all the food elements to make good blood.

REMEMBER, include in the diet a wide variety of fruits and vegetables, dark leafy greens, more raw foods, whole grain cereals and breads, vegetable proteins from sources such as dry beans, peas, and other legumes (soybeans, garbanzos, kidney, pintos, lentils, etc.), tofu, nuts, seeds, and soybean milk. Our recommendations are a high starch, low fat, and moderate protein diet that includes plenty of raw fruits and vegetables.

Reduce the fats, oils, salt, and sugars in the diet and avoid high cholesterol foods such as eggs, cheese, butter, and meats. All animal foods contain cholesterol, and that includes chicken and fish. Let the diet reform be progressive! Paul says in 1 Corinthians 6:19,20, and 10:31:

"What? Know ye not that your body is the temple of the Holy Ghost which is in you, which ye have of God, and ye are not your own?"

"For ye are bought with a price: therefore glorify God in your body, and in your spirit, which are God's." "Whatever you eat or drink, or whatever you do, do it all for the glory of God."

## 8—TRUST IN DIVINE POWER
"And the rib, which the Lord God had taken from man, made He a woman, and brought her unto the man." Gen. 2:22

Who is the Great Physician?

"For without faith it is impossible to please Him, for he that cometh to God must believe that he is, and that He is a rewarder of them that diligently seek Him." Heb. 11:6

Where does all healing come from?

"Trust in the Lord with all thine heart, and lean not unto thine own understanding....it shall be health to thy navel, and marrow to thy bones." Prov. 3:5, 8

What is His desire for your life?

"Beloved, I wish above all things that you may prosper and be in health, even as your soul prospereth." 3 John 2

Does He want our complete restoration?

"And the very God of peace sanctify you wholly; and I pray God your whole spirit and soul and body be preserved blameless unto the coming of our Lord Jesus Christ." 1 Thess. 5:23

Does a lack of trust create a negative influence?

"A merry heart does good like a medicine: but a broken spirit dries the bones." Prov. 17:22

"A sound heart is the life of the flesh; but envy the rottenness of the bones." Prov. 14:30

Remember, worry, stress, and depression = decay, disease, and death. The immune system is strengthened by trusting God.

The foundation of all health is in the acceptance of the blessings which the Creator has provided for us. Foremost of these is the privilege we have of our Heavenly Father being our Guide as well as our Great Physician. Our physical healing is with the purpose of making us more inclined to accept the spiritual healing Christ longs to perform upon our hearts.

There is an inexpressible peace that comes to one who has learned to trust in God, and lay all things in His hands. Jesus says, "Come unto Me, and I will give you rest." Matthew 11:28...rest from sorrow, rest from fear, rest from insecurity. But first we must come to Him. As our Great Physician, we must trust Him to know His profession. Trust in His wisdom and love. Then resign ourselves to do His will, and endeavor faithfully to follow every instruction He gives. When we come to God, we must be willing to acknowledge and accept His ways as best for us, and follow them, regardless of our own personal preference and prejudices. At times, we may not discern

126

His wisdom in certain events, and it is then that we honor Him by our faith. By being obedient to Him in those things which He asks of us—be it in the physical or spiritual realm—we must trust that He will guide us on our way to complete healing.

"Keep your wants, your joys, your sorrows, your cares, and your fears before God…. The Lord is very pitiful and of tender mercy. James 5:11. His heart of love is touched by our sorrows and even by our utterance of them…. Nothing that in any way concerns our peace is too small for Him to notice. There is no chapter in our experience too dark for Him to read. There is no perplexity too difficult for Him to unravel. No calamity can befall the least of His children, no anxiety harass the soul, no joy or cheer, no sincere prayer escape the lips, of which our Heavenly Father is unobservant, or in which He takes no immediate interest. 'He heals the brokenhearted and binds up their wounds.' Psalm 147:3." SC pg. 100

Your Prescription for a successful lifestyle: "Through nature and revelation, through His providence, and by the influence of the Holy Spirit, God speaks to us. But these are not enough; we need also to pour out our hearts to Him. In order to have spiritual life and energy, we must have actual intercourse with our heavenly Father.

"Prayer is the opening of the heart to God as to a friend…. Prayer does not bring God down to us, but brings us up to Him.

"Jesus found comfort and joy in communion with His Father. And if the Saviour of men, the Son of God, felt the need of prayer, how much much more should feeble, sinful mortals feel the necessity of fervent, constant prayer." SC pp. 64, 65

"Behold, I stand at the door and knock: if any man hear My voice, and open the door, I will come in and sup with him, and he with Me." Revelation 3:20

In conclusion may we never forget:

"And the Lord commanded us to do all these statutes, to fear the Lord our God, for our good always, that He might **preserve us alive,** as it is at this day." Deut. 7:24

---

[1]Living for Health, Margaretha Eales

# Index

## Italian

## Mexican

## Patties, Meatballs, & Breads

## Potato Dishes

# Modern Manna Video Series

Invite your friends to enjoy four nights of a
**Vegetarian Cooking School and Lecture Series**

*Up-to-date information on*
- *benefits of a vegetarian diet*
- *lifestyle for excellent health*
- *recipe preparation and menus*
- *permanent weight loss*
- *lowering cholesterol*
- *triglyceride control*
- *health principles from the Bible*

*Includes videos each night on health and animal slaughter.*

An Excellent "entering wedge." for your friends, old and new!

Now you can conduct your own vegetarian Cooking school, Showing one video each night and demonstrating the recipes using the cookbook as your syllabus.

---

**Order your videos and
cookbook today!**

4 Videos and a copy of the
**Vegetarian Cooking School
Cookbook**
For only $75.00
($5.00 shipping & handling)

**Danny & Charise Vierra**
519 S. Central Avenue
Lodi, CA 95240
**(209) 368-3168**